CANNON W. STIFFLER

My Mind Struggles

First edition

Editing by Candice Weddington

This book was professionally typeset on Reedsy.
Find out more at reedsy.com

Contents

Author's Note v
Acknowledgments vii

I MEMOIR

1 Me Before 3
2 The Stranger in the Mirror 9
3 Living Behind Glass 34
4 The Weight of the Storm 43
5 The Watching Mind 48
6 The Quiet Between 57
7 Mind Isn't Mine 72
8 Aftermath 86
9 Inside My Mind 92
10 Mad Mind 108
11 What I Learned 148
12 … 159

II PSYCHOEDUCATION

13 Anger Management 163
14 Healthy Relationships 168
15 Guilt & Shame 172
16 Self-Compassion 176

17 Schemas 180
18 Cognitive Behavioral Therapy 183
19 Mindfulness 188
20 Adequacy 193
21 Schema Modes 197
22 Early Maladaptive Schemas (EMS) 202
23 Schema Avoidance (EAs / Coping Styles) 207
24 Core Beliefs 211
25 5 Schema Domains 215
26 Good Parent Letter 221
27 Emotions 101 225
28 Occupational Therapy Education 230
29 Authenticity 235
30 Hope 240
31 Unhealthy Relationships 245
32 Trust 249
33 Boundaries 254
34 Assertiveness 259
35 Stigma 264
36 Symptom Management 269
37 Co-Dependency 274
38 Dependency 279
39 Independency 283
40 Interdependency 287
41 Grief & Loss 291

A Letter to You 296
Notes From a Full Mind 301
When Your Mind Gets Too Loud 305
About the Author 307

Author's Note

This book isn't meant to be a clinical explanation or a perfect timeline of recovery or advice of any kind. It's a lived experience—messy, nonlinear, and still ongoing in many ways. What I've tried to capture here is not just what it feels like to struggle internally but what it feels like to learn how to stay present inside that struggle without letting it define everything.

If you recognize parts of yourself in these pages, I want you to know you're not alone in that experience. Internal overwhelm, disconnection, anxiety, or feeling detached from yourself can feel isolating, especially when it's hard to explain to other people. But those experiences don't make you weak, broken, or less than anyone else. They make you human in a way that is often difficult to put into words.

One of the biggest lessons I've learned is that healing is not a straight line. It doesn't look like constant improvement, and it doesn't mean never feeling the same things again. For me, it has looked more like learning how to respond differently over time—how to come back to myself faster, how to stop turning every moment into a conclusion, and how to allow experiences to pass without losing myself inside them.

I also want to acknowledge something important that I believe needs to be said clearly: people who struggle deeply, including those who reach points of self-harm or suicide, are not weak. They are often carrying more internal pain than others can see or understand. Weakness is not found in suffering. Weakness is in how easily people can be dismissed, judged, or shamed for what they are going through instead of being met with compassion and understanding.

If anything, this story is a reminder that survival—of any kind—is not small. Even the quiet kind. Even the unseen kind.

And for anyone who is still in the middle of it right now: you don't have to have everything figured out to keep going. You don't have to feel fully okay in order to continue. You don't have to become someone else to deserve support or understanding. I use past tense and present tense throughout the pages that follow—don't let it fool you. I write some of these past-tense verbs with hope to overcome them. I write the present-tense verbs because I can always feel them—no matter how minor.

Remember:

You are already allowed to stay.

And that matters.

Acknowledgments

To the versions of me that didn't know how to explain what was happening but kept going anyway—thank you. This book exists because you didn't stop.

To anyone who has ever felt like their mind was too loud, too distant, too uncertain, or too difficult to understand—your experience is real, even when it's hard to describe.

And to the people who choose empathy over judgment, even when they don't fully understand what someone else is going through—this world needs more of you than it realizes.

I

MEMOIR

1

Me Before

Memory is a strange thing.

The older I get, the less I remember specific days and the more I remember feelings. Childhood exists in fragments now—sunlight pouring through a car window, the smell of freshly cut grass drifting through an open window, the sound of laughter bouncing through a neighborhood on a summer evening, and the feeling of running until my lungs burned because stopping simply wasn't an option. The details have softened with time. Faces blur. Dates disappear. Entire years collapse into a handful of moments. Yet somehow the feeling of being that person remains. It lingers in the corners of my memory like an old photograph that has faded around the edges but still tells the same story.

When I think about the version of me that existed before all of this, I don't think about diagnoses or symptoms. I think about moments.

I think about my grandpa having bright pink hair and nobody acting like it was unusual. Looking back, it sounds ridiculous. At the time, it was just Grandpa. I think about coming out of daycare one afternoon and finding a SpongeBob car seat my dad had bought for me. To anyone else, it was just a car seat. To me, it felt like Christmas had arrived without warning. I think about sitting at a tiny table during a tea party with my mom at daycare, both of us drinking lemon tea out of teacups. Those were the most important things in the world. I think about my sister accidentally burning me with a heating lamp in the garage. It hurt then. Now it's one of those stories that makes me laugh.

Those are the memories that survived.

Not because they were extraordinary.

Because they were mine.

One thing you'll learn about me quickly is that I hated being inside. If there was a chance to be outdoors, that's where I wanted to be. I spent countless hours running around my neighborhood with friends, turning roads into racetracks and patches of woods into unexplored territory. Every day felt like it held the possibility of an adventure, even if that adventure was nothing more than riding bikes until the streetlights came on.

Some of my favorite memories were spent in the creeks around my house. My friends and I would search along the muddy banks, lifting rocks and looking for crawdads. Looking back, I don't think it was ever really about finding them. It was about the hunt. It was about having nowhere else to be and all day to get there. Childhood has a way of making ordinary things feel important, and at the time there was nothing ordinary about it. We weren't kids standing in a creek. We were explorers discovering something nobody had ever seen before.

The world felt bigger then.

I was also the kind of kid who always had something to say. Quiet was never my natural state. I liked talking. I liked being involved. I liked knowing what was going on and being part of it. If there was a conversation happening, chances were I wanted to join it. If there was a game being played, I wanted in.

And if there was a competition, I wanted to win.

I hated losing.

Not because I wanted to be better than everyone else, but because I cared. Whether it was a board game, a race, or some challenge my friends and I had invented five minutes earlier, I wanted to win. I threw myself into things completely. Looking back now, I think that's because I was fully present in my life. I wasn't standing on the sidelines watching it happen. I was in it.

School was another place where I felt at home. I know that sounds strange because most people spend their childhood counting down the days until summer break. But I loved school. I loved having somewhere to be every day. I loved having a purpose. I loved seeing my friends, learning new things, and having a routine. Looking back, I realize school gave me something I wouldn't fully appreciate until years later—it occupied my mind.

My thoughts weren't my focus.

Life was.

Every morning there was somewhere to go, someone to see, and something to do. I didn't spend time analyzing every thought that crossed my mind because I was too busy living.

When I think about my childhood, I think about family, too.

I think about Saturdays spent at my Grandma Coco's house.

It was one of those places that felt permanent when you were a kid, as though nothing inside it could ever change. The adults would talk while I found ways to entertain myself, and somehow those days always felt longer than they actually were. Safe. Familiar. Predictable.

I think about my dad.

My dad died in a car accident when I was six years old. People sometimes assume that means I have endless stories about him. The truth is that I don't. I was young, and time has a way of carrying memories away. There are things I wish I remembered. Conversations I wish I could hear again. Moments I wish I could revisit.

But memory doesn't always work the way we want it to.

What remains are fragments.

I remember my dad and I having matching mohawks. Out of all the things time could have taken, that's one of the things it left behind. I remember thinking it was the coolest thing in the world. I remember feeling proud to match him.

I remember my grandpa's red Dodge truck.

I remember my dad driving it.

I couldn't tell you every place we went or every conversation we had inside that truck. I couldn't tell you what song was playing on the radio or what the weather was like outside. What I remember is the feeling of it. The comfort. The normalcy. The way certain memories become attached to ordinary objects and refuse to let go.

It's strange what time decides to keep.

There are entire years that feel blurry now, yet somehow I can still picture that red truck.

As I've gotten older, I've realized that the things I miss most about childhood aren't the major events. They're the ordinary moments that seemed too small to matter at the time. The moments nobody tells you to hold onto because nobody realizes they'll become memories one day.

The car rides.

The afternoons outside.

The tea parties.

Creek water soaking through my shoes.

The laughter.

The conversations.

The feeling that tomorrow would arrive looking more or less like today.

What I miss most about the person I was before all of this isn't that he was happier. Life wasn't perfect. It never is. I lost my dad. I had difficult days. I worried about things. I got hurt. I got embarrassed. I made mistakes.

What I miss is the certainty.

I trusted my mind.

I trusted reality.

I trusted that the world around me was exactly what it appeared to be.

I never worried about whether I felt connected to my surroundings. I never questioned whether I felt real. The idea itself would have sounded absurd to me. My mind wasn't something I studied or analyzed. It was simply home.

Looking back, that feels like a gift.

For thirteen years, I lived without realizing how valuable that certainty was. I assumed everyone felt the same way I did. I assumed reality would always feel real. I assumed my thoughts would always feel familiar. I assumed my mind would always be a place I could trust.

Then, somewhere around thirteen years old, something

changed.

I wish I could tell you there was a specific day.

A specific moment.

A line dividing before and after.

But there wasn't.

If there was a beginning, it was quiet enough that I almost missed it.

At first, it was just a feeling.

A feeling I couldn't explain.

A feeling I couldn't name.

A feeling that something wasn't quite right.

I didn't know it then, but the place that had always felt safest—my own mind—was about to become unfamiliar.

2

The Stranger in the Mirror

There is a difference between feeling that something is wrong and feeling that something has broken. For a long time, I couldn't tell which side of that line I was standing on. Looking back now, I think I spent years slowly walking toward it without realizing it was there. The strange thing about mental health is that it rarely arrives all at once. It doesn't usually kick down the front door and announce itself. More often, it slips quietly through a crack in the wall and makes itself at home before you even notice it's there. By the time you realize something has changed, it's already been changing for a while.

Even now, I sometimes find myself wondering when my struggle truly began. Was it when anxiety first became more than ordinary worry? Was it when depression started settling into places I couldn't reach? Was it when I began questioning thoughts that had never bothered me before? I don't know. What I do know is that by the spring of 2026, I was carrying more than I realized. Anxiety had become a constant companion. Depression was beginning to creep back into my life. Stress sat on my shoulders so often that I stopped noticing its weight. From the outside, I was still functioning. I went to school. I talked to people. I made plans. I laughed when I was supposed to laugh. If you had looked at me from across a room, you probably wouldn't have seen anything unusual. That's one of the cruelest things about invisible struggles: they are often invisible even to the person carrying them.

I had convinced myself I was okay because I was still moving forward. Looking back, I understand how flawed that logic was. A person can be drowning and still appear calm from the shore. A person can be falling apart while continuing to show up every day. A person can become so accustomed to surviving that they forget living is supposed to feel different. Somewhere along the way, I had become emotionally exhausted. Not physically tired, but worn down in a way sleep could never fix. Every day felt like carrying a backpack full of invisible bricks. Anxiety added one. Depression added another. Fear added another. Over time, the weight became part of me. I stopped asking whether it was heavy because I couldn't remember what it felt like to carry nothing at all.

Then came April 17, 2026.

I remember the date because there are certain days that split your life into before and after. Not because the world changes, but because your relationship with it does. Before that weekend, I believed my mind was a place I could trust. It wasn't perfect, but it was familiar. It was home. After that weekend, something shifted. The place I had always felt safest suddenly felt unfamiliar, and that terrified me more than anything else ever had.

The night itself wasn't remarkable. There wasn't an emergency. There wasn't a tragedy. There wasn't a dramatic event that would later explain everything. That's part of what makes the memory so unsettling. If there had been a clear cause, I could have pointed to it. I could have built a story around it. Instead, what happened seemed to come entirely from within me. One moment I was sitting with my own thoughts. Next, I felt something I had never felt before. Something I've never seen before.

At first, it was difficult to describe. Truthfully, it still is. Some experiences seem to exist beyond language. Every explanation feels too small. Every metaphor leaves something behind. The closest I can come is this: I felt trapped inside my own existence. Suddenly, I became intensely aware of the fact that I was alive. Aware that I was thinking. Aware that I was conscious. Aware that I existed. Those facts had always been true, but they had never felt frightening before. Now they did. I saw myself, lying in my bed—from the third point-of-view.

The feeling grew quickly. What started as discomfort became fear, and what started as fear became panic. The world around me looked exactly the same, yet it no longer felt the same. Everything seemed distant, dreamlike, and strangely artificial. I knew where I was. I knew who I was. I knew the world was real. Yet emotionally, it felt as though a wall had appeared between me and everything around me. It was like looking through glass that nobody else could see.

I remember trying to make sense of it. I remember trying to reason with it. I remember desperately searching for an explanation that would make the feeling disappear. Instead, my thoughts only seemed to multiply. One question became five. Five became twenty. Soon my mind was racing faster than I could keep up with it.

What if something is wrong with me?

What if I stay like this?

What if this never goes away?

For the first time in my life, I wasn't afraid of something outside of me.

I was afraid of my own mind.

And I had no idea that the worst was still a few days away.

Tuesday night arrived carrying all of the fear I had accumulated over the previous few days. By then, I had become obsessed with understanding what had happened to me. Every free moment was spent researching symptoms, reading stories, and searching for answers. The problem was that every answer seemed to create another question. Instead of finding reassurance, I found myself trapped in an endless cycle of analysis. I was constantly checking how I felt, constantly evaluating whether I felt normal, constantly monitoring my own thoughts. Looking back, I realize that anxiety had turned my attention inward. Instead of living my life, I had begun observing it. Instead of experiencing reality, I was evaluating my experience of reality. By the time Tuesday night arrived, I was exhausted in a way that sleep couldn't fix.

I don't remember every detail of that evening, but I remember the mirror. I've looked into mirrors thousands of times throughout my life without giving them a second thought. That night, however, something felt different. I remember standing there looking at my reflection and feeling a wave of discomfort that I couldn't explain. The face staring back at me was mine. I knew it was mine. There was never a moment where I genuinely believed otherwise. Yet the connection felt weaker somehow, as though a thin sheet of glass had appeared between me and the person looking back. The longer I stared, the stranger the experience became. My eyes looked familiar. My face looked familiar. Every feature was exactly where it had always been. Nothing had changed, and yet everything felt different. I stood there searching for a feeling that refused to arrive, trying to convince myself that I was okay while simultaneously becoming more frightened by the second. When I finally walked away, the fear followed me. It followed me into bed. It followed me into the darkness. It followed me into every thought I had as I lay there trying to fall asleep.

Sleep eventually came, but it wasn't the escape I had been hoping for. By the time I finally drifted off, I was exhausted in a way that went far beyond being tired. My mind had spent days running in circles, replaying fears, searching for answers, and trying to understand something that felt impossible to explain. I remember hoping that sleep would somehow reset everything. Maybe I would wake up and feel normal again. Maybe whatever had happened to me would feel smaller in the morning. Maybe the fear would finally loosen its grip. Instead, when morning arrived, it brought something much worse.

I woke up sometime around five o'clock. The house was silent, still wrapped in the darkness that exists just before sunrise. For a few moments, I wasn't fully awake. I lingered somewhere between dreaming and consciousness, caught in that strange place where reality hasn't completely settled back into focus. Then, almost immediately, a feeling washed over me. To this day, I struggle to explain exactly what happened because some parts of that morning remain vivid while others feel distorted by fear and time. What I remember most clearly is the overwhelming sense that I needed to check on my mom. It wasn't a normal thought. It didn't feel like simple concern. It felt urgent, almost instinctive, as though some invisible alarm had gone off inside my mind. The feeling was so strong that it cut through everything else.

When I sat up, panic hit me with a force I had never experienced before. It felt as though every fear I had been carrying over the previous days suddenly arrived at the same time. My heart raced. My thoughts scattered. The room around me was the same room I had fallen asleep in, my mom's room, only hours earlier, yet it felt unfamiliar in a way that is difficult to describe. I knew where I was. I knew who I was. I knew who she, my mom, was. I knew that everything around me was real. Yet none of that knowledge seemed capable of calming me. Reality itself felt fragile, as though the certainty I had always relied on had suddenly disappeared. Every sensation felt amplified. Every thought seemed significant. My mind searched desperately for something solid to hold onto and found nothing.

I sat there trying to convince myself that I was okay, but reassurance seemed to dissolve the moment I reached for it. The more I tried to reason with myself, the worse the fear became. Looking back now, I understand that my nervous system was likely overwhelmed. My body was reacting as though I were facing some immediate threat even though no threat existed. At the time, however, I wasn't thinking about anxiety or adrenaline or panic responses. I wasn't thinking about any of the explanations I would later learn. I was thinking one thing and one thing only: something is wrong with me; I'm going to die. That thought consumed everything else. For days, I had been searching for answers.

For days, I had been trying to convince myself that what I experienced was temporary. Now every terrifying possibility seemed to rush into the empty spaces where certainty used to live.

The questions came faster than I could answer them. What if this isn't anxiety? What if something is seriously wrong? What if I never feel normal again? What if this is who I am now? The thoughts piled on top of each other until I could barely separate one from the next. Every attempt to fight them seemed to make them stronger. Every effort to regain control only reminded me how little control I felt I had. It was as though my mind had become a room full of mirrors, each one reflecting fear back at me from a different angle.

Eventually, I tried to get out of bed because sitting there felt impossible. Staying still with my thoughts felt impossible. Everything felt impossible. I remember wanting relief more than anything else. I wanted someone to tell me what was happening. I wanted someone to tell me that I would be okay. I wanted a guarantee that the version of myself I had always known was still somewhere inside me. Instead, I found myself sitting on the edge of my mom's bed repetitively taking my BP in my mom's room, feeling disconnected from everything that had once felt familiar and freaking out because the BP machine would light my face red. For the first time in my life, my own mind felt like a place I didn't recognize, and that realization terrified me more than anything that had happened before.

At that moment, I didn't know that the morning was only beginning. I didn't know that within the next—what felt like an hour—five minutes I would find myself sitting on the floor trying to get dressed because standing felt impossible.

I didn't know that fear was about to push me to a place I never imagined I would go. All I knew was that I was scared, exhausted, and desperately searching for a way back to myself.

What happened next remains one of the clearest memories from that entire period of my life. Trauma has a strange way of preserving certain moments. Entire days can disappear, yet five minutes can remain untouched for years. I don't remember every detail of that morning, but I remember the feeling. I remember the fear. I remember the overwhelming sense that something inside me had shifted and that I no longer knew how to shift it back.

Getting dressed should have been simple. It was something I had done thousands of times without thinking. That morning, however, even the smallest tasks felt impossible. I remember sitting on the floor because standing felt wrong. Every time I tried to get up, I felt unstable, as though my body and mind were no longer communicating properly. My thoughts were moving so quickly that I could barely keep track of them, and my body seemed determined to follow their chaos. I would stand, lose my balance, and catch myself against the wall. Then I would sit back down and try again. Something as ordinary as putting on clothes had become a struggle.

What scared me most wasn't the dizziness or the panic. It was how unfamiliar everything felt. The room was mine—spinning but mine. The clothes were mine. The life waiting for me outside that bedroom door was mine. Yet I felt disconnected from all of it. It was as though I had become an observer inside my own life. I could see everything. I could recognize everything. I simply couldn't feel connected to it in the way I always had before. That disconnect terrified me because I couldn't explain it. I couldn't point to a wound.

I couldn't point to an illness. I couldn't point to anything concrete and say, "That's the problem." All I had was a feeling, and that feeling was consuming me.

As I sat on that floor, my mind continued doing what it had been doing for days: searching for explanations. Every possibility seemed worse than the last. I wondered if I was losing control. I wondered if I was losing myself. I wondered if this was permanent. Looking back now, I understand that fear was writing stories faster than reality could keep up with them. Anxiety has a way of turning uncertainty into catastrophe. It sees a question mark and immediately replaces it with the worst possible answer. At the time, though, I didn't know that. I believed every frightening thought deserved my attention. I treated every fear as evidence.

The hardest part to explain is how alone I felt despite being surrounded by people who cared about me. Anxiety can be incredibly isolating because so much of the battle takes place inside your own head. From the outside, people see someone who is scared. They see someone who is struggling. What they don't see is the constant conversation happening underneath. They don't hear the questions. They don't feel the uncertainty. They don't experience the relentless cycle of fear feeding more fear. I remember feeling trapped inside that cycle, unable to imagine what it would feel like to be free from it.

Eventually, it became clear that this was bigger than something I could simply push through. Up until that point, I had spent most of my life believing that if I just thought hard enough, worked hard enough, or stayed strong enough, I could overcome whatever was in front of me. This felt different. The more I fought it alone, the worse it seemed to become. For the first time, I found myself facing a problem that couldn't be solved through determination alone. I needed help.

That realization was difficult to accept. Part of me wanted to believe I could handle everything myself. Part of me wanted to wake up and discover that this had all been a misunderstanding. But another part of me—the exhausted part, the terrified part—knew that I couldn't keep carrying this by myself. The fear had become too heavy. The uncertainty had become too loud. I needed answers, and more importantly, I needed support.

By the time we decided to go to the Behavioral Health Crisis Center at Ohio State, I felt completely drained. Fear had been running through my system for days. My mind had spent countless hours imagining worst-case scenarios. My body felt exhausted from constantly preparing for danger that never arrived. As we made our way there, I remember staring out the window and wondering how I had gotten to this point. Just days earlier, my biggest concern had been trying to understand what had happened during that first episode. Now I was on my way to a crisis center because I no longer trusted my ability to navigate it alone.

I wish I could say I felt relief.

I didn't.

I felt scared.

Scared of what they might tell me.

Scared of what they might find.

Scared that somehow all of my worst fears would be confirmed.

At the same time, buried beneath all that fear was something else. Something small, but important.

Hope.

Because for the first time since this all began, I wasn't

searching for answers by myself anymore.

The drive there felt longer than it probably was. Fear has a way of stretching time, turning minutes into hours and making every thought feel heavier than the last. I remember staring out the window, watching the world continue as if nothing had changed. Cars moved through intersections. People walked into stores. Traffic lights cycled from red to green and back again. Everything looked normal. Everything looked exactly the same as it had the week before.

I envied that.

Not the cars or the traffic lights, but the feeling of normal. The feeling of moving through life without questioning every thought. The feeling of existing without constantly checking whether existence itself felt real. As I watched the world pass by, I remember wondering how everyone else seemed to do it so effortlessly. How were people laughing, working, making plans, and living their lives while I felt trapped inside my own mind? It seemed impossible that the world could continue moving at its usual pace while mine felt completely frozen.

By the time we arrived, I was emotionally exhausted. Fear had become my default setting. Every thought seemed to pass through a filter of anxiety before it reached me. Every sensation felt significant. Every emotion felt dangerous. I remember walking inside and feeling exposed, as though everyone around me could somehow see everything I had been carrying. Looking back, I know that wasn't true. The people there had likely seen hundreds of people struggling with their own battles. At the time, however, it felt as though I was walking into the building carrying every fear I had ever had.

One of the strangest things about that day was realizing I

wasn't the only person there.

That sounds obvious now, but at the time it mattered.

For days, I had felt completely alone. Even when I was surrounded by people who loved me, there was still a part of me that believed nobody could possibly understand what was happening inside my head. The fear felt too specific. Too strange. Too difficult to explain. Yet sitting there, I began to understand something that anxiety had been hiding from me: struggling did not make me unique. It made me human.

I wasn't the first person whose mind had frightened them.

I wouldn't be the last.

That realization didn't magically fix anything. I didn't walk through those doors and suddenly feel normal again. I still don't. I didn't receive a perfect explanation that made every fear disappear. And still don't. Recovery doesn't work that way, no matter how badly we wish it did. And it still doesn't. What I found instead was something far more important.

I found people who weren't afraid of what I was experiencing.

For days, I had been treating every thought like an emergency. Every symptom felt catastrophic. Every fear felt urgent. My mind had convinced me that I was standing on the edge of something terrible. Yet the people helping me weren't panicking. They weren't reacting as though I was beyond saving. They weren't looking at me like I had become someone else.

To them, I was a person who was struggling.

Nothing more.

Nothing less.

Looking back, that may have been one of the most important moments of the entire journey. Anxiety had spent days convincing me that I was broken beyond recognition. It had convinced me that something unimaginable was happening to me. Sitting there, listening to people speak calmly about experiences that felt impossible to survive, I began to realize that maybe my fear had been telling a larger story than reality was.

That didn't mean the fear disappeared.

It didn't.

I still felt disconnected.

I still felt terrified.

I still questioned myself constantly.

But for the first time since that Friday night, there was a small crack in the certainty of my fear. A small opening where hope could begin to exist.

The truth was that I wanted an answer.

I wanted someone to point to a chart, a scan, a diagnosis, or a single sentence and explain everything. I wanted certainty because certainty felt like safety. Unfortunately, healing rarely begins with certainty. More often, it begins with accepting uncertainty and continuing forward anyway.

I didn't know that yet.

All I knew was that I was tired.

Tired of researching.

Tired of checking.

Tired of analyzing every thought that entered my mind.

Tired of being afraid.

For nearly a week, I had been fighting an invisible battle every waking moment. Even when I wasn't actively thinking about it, part of my brain remained on guard, waiting for the next wave of fear to arrive. Living that way was exhausting. It felt like running a marathon without ever reaching a finish line.

As the day continued, I found myself reflecting on a question I had been avoiding ever since this began.

What if I weren't losing my mind?

The thought felt foreign.

Almost uncomfortable.

Fear had spent so much time convincing me of the worst possible outcomes that considering a different possibility felt strange. What if this wasn't the end of my life as I knew it? What if this wasn't permanent? What if the terrifying thoughts weren't predictions at all?

What if they were symptoms?

For the first time, I allowed myself to consider that possibility.

Not fully.

Not confidently.

Just enough.

And although I couldn't feel it then, that small shift in perspective would eventually become the first step toward finding my way back.

Because the truth was that something had changed inside me.

But the truth was also this:

I was still there.

Buried beneath the fear, beneath the panic, beneath the endless questions and sleepless nights, I was still there.

I just hadn't found my way back to myself yet.

And that journey was only beginning.

When I think back on that week, I don't remember it as a series of events. I remember it as a feeling. A heavy, suffocating feeling that seemed to follow me everywhere

I went. Before all of this happened, I believed fear was something that appeared in moments. You get scared, the moment passes, and eventually life returns to normal. What I didn't understand was that fear can become a place. It can become an environment you live inside. It can follow you into classrooms, into conversations, into car rides, into the quiet moments before sleep. Even after leaving Ohio State, even after speaking to people who understood what I was experiencing better than I did, I still carried that fear with me. The difference was that now I also carried something else: the possibility that I wasn't broken beyond repair.

That possibility felt fragile. Some days it was barely noticeable. Fear was still louder. Fear was still faster. Fear still had a response for every reassuring thought I managed to find. If I told myself that people recover from experiences like this, fear would immediately ask, "What if you're different?" If I reminded myself that anxiety can create powerful symptoms, fear would respond, "What if this isn't anxiety?" It seemed as though every answer led to another question. Every attempt at reassurance became another opportunity for doubt. Looking back now, I realize I wasn't fighting reality. I was fighting uncertainty. I wanted guarantees. I wanted certainty that I would feel normal again. I wanted certainty that I wasn't losing my mind. I wanted certainty that life would eventually return to the way it had been before. The problem was that certainty isn't something life often offers us.

The days that followed became an exhausting cycle of observation. I watched my own thoughts constantly. I watched my emotions. I watched my reactions. I watched reality itself. Every experience seemed to come with a silent evaluation. Does this feel normal? Do I feel connected enough? Does this feel real enough? Am I okay? Looking back, it's difficult to explain how much energy that consumed. Most people experience life directly. I felt as though I was experiencing life through a layer of analysis. Instead of simply living, I was studying my own existence. Instead of participating in moments, I was evaluating them. It was like trying to enjoy a movie while simultaneously examining every frame under a microscope. Eventually, the analysis becomes all you can see.

There were moments when I genuinely wondered if I would ever feel like myself again. That's one of the hardest parts to admit because I know how dramatic it sounds. But when you're in the middle of something like that, your perspective changes. A week feels like a year. A month feels impossible to imagine. The version of yourself that existed before the struggle begins to feel distant, almost like someone you used to know rather than someone you still are. I missed the simplicity of my old life. I missed waking up without immediately checking how I felt. I missed being able to look in a mirror without questioning my reflection. I missed existing without constantly thinking about existence. Most of all, I missed trusting my own mind.

The cruel irony is that the harder I searched for proof that I was okay, the harder it became to feel okay. Anxiety is strange that way. It promises certainty if you'll just keep checking one more time. One more symptom search. One more article. One more mental test. One more attempt to figure everything out. The problem is that the finish line never arrives. Every answer creates another question, and every question creates another opportunity for fear. I didn't understand that yet. At the time, I still believed there was some magical piece of information waiting for me somewhere. Some sentence that would suddenly make everything click into place and restore my peace of mind.

There wasn't.

What I would eventually learn is that recovery wasn't going to come from solving every question. It wasn't going to come from finding perfect certainty. It wasn't going to come from winning an argument against fear. Recovery would come much later, through things I couldn't yet see and lessons I hadn't yet learned. At that moment, however, I was still standing at the beginning of the journey. I was still frightened. I was still confused. I was still carrying more questions than answers. But somewhere beneath all of that, buried deep beneath the panic and uncertainty, something had survived.

Hope.

Not a loud hope. Not a confident hope. Not the kind that suddenly transforms a person's life.

Just enough hope to keep moving.

And sometimes, that is where healing begins.

Looking back now, I think one of the most difficult parts of that season of my life was accepting that there wasn't going to be a dramatic ending. Nobody sat me down and handed me a map. There wasn't a single appointment that made everything make sense. There wasn't a morning where I woke up and suddenly felt like the version of myself that had existed before April. Part of me expected recovery to feel obvious. I expected there to be a moment where I could point to a calendar and say, "That's when things got better." Instead, what I found was something far less satisfying and far more real. Life kept moving. The sun kept rising. School continued. Assignments piled up. Conversations happened. The world refused to stop simply because I was struggling to understand what was happening inside my own mind.

That was frustrating at first. There is a part of suffering that wants the world to acknowledge it. Not out of selfishness, but because pain feels so large when you're carrying it that it becomes difficult to understand how everything else can continue as normal. I remember sitting in classrooms and looking around at the people beside me, wondering how they were able to focus on ordinary things. How were they worried about homework, sports, weekend plans, and upcoming tests when I felt trapped inside questions that seemed infinitely larger? How could life continue feeling ordinary for everyone else when my own reality felt as though it had been shaken loose from its foundation? Of course, what I didn't understand at the time was that everyone is carrying something. Not necessarily the same thing, not necessarily something visible, but something. Pain has a way of convincing us that we're isolated in our experience when, in reality, struggle is one of the most universal parts of being human.

The fear didn't disappear after Ohio State, even after the four-week intense program I went through. It took a long long time to even remember what life without fear felt like, and to be honest, I still don't fully have that grasped. If anything, it simply changed shape. At first, I had been terrified of the experience itself. Then I became terrified of experiencing it again. Those fears sound similar, but they're different. The panic attack was an event. The anticipation of another panic attack became a lifestyle. Every day felt like waiting for something to happen. Every strange sensation made me nervous. Every moment of anxiety immediately grabbed my attention. I became hyper-aware of everything happening inside my own head. If my thoughts felt different, I noticed. If my emotions felt different, I noticed. If reality felt even slightly strange, I noticed. It got so bad that I believed that coincidences were caused by the simulation we lived in (sometimes I still think this). My attention had become permanently fixed on myself, and that level of self-awareness was exhausting. It's difficult to explain to someone who hasn't experienced it. Imagine constantly monitoring your own breathing. At first it's manageable. Eventually it's all you can think about. That's what life began to feel like.

What frightened me most wasn't the panic itself. It was the possibility that I would never stop thinking about it. There were moments when I became afraid that this was simply who I was now. Maybe this was my life. Maybe every day would begin with checking how I felt. Maybe every thought would have to be analyzed. Maybe every moment would come attached to a question mark. Those fears often felt heavier than the symptoms themselves because they reached into the future and tried to convince me it was already written. Anxiety has a remarkable talent for pretending it can predict tomorrow. It speaks in certainties. It tells you what will happen, what won't happen, what you'll never overcome, and what you'll never escape. The problem is that anxiety is a terrible fortune teller. It speaks with complete confidence and almost no accuracy.

At the time, however, I didn't know that—and honestly, I still don't sometimes. I'm still learning. Still trying to separate fear from fact. Still trying to understand the difference between a feeling and a reality. Every day seemed to present a new challenge. Some days I felt almost normal, only to have the fear return stronger the next day. Other days I felt exhausted before I even got out of bed. There was no consistency. No roadmap. No clear indication of whether I was moving forward or backward. That uncertainty frustrated me because I wanted progress to be measurable. I wanted recovery to work like a broken bone. You get hurt, you heal, and eventually you're better. Mental health doesn't operate that way. Healing is often invisible while it's happening. Sometimes you don't notice you've made progress until you look back months later and realize you're standing somewhere you once thought you'd never reach.

At the end of that week, I didn't feel victorious. I didn't feel cured. I didn't even feel particularly hopeful. Mostly, I felt tired. Tired of being scared. Tired of searching for answers. Tired of carrying questions that never seemed to stay answered. Yet beneath that exhaustion was something important. For the first time since all of this began, I had stopped asking whether I would survive it. The question had quietly changed. Instead of wondering if I would make it through, I had started wondering how I would make it through. It wasn't a dramatic shift, and I didn't recognize it at the time. Looking back, though, I think it mattered more than I realized. Because the moment you begin asking "how" instead of "if," you've already taken your first step toward the other side.

I didn't know it then, but the battle that had begun inside my own mind was far from over. There would be more fear. More questions. More sleepless nights. More moments where reality felt distant and my own thoughts felt overwhelming. There would also be lessons, growth, answers, and people who would help carry me through the parts I couldn't carry alone. The story wasn't ending.

In many ways, it was only beginning.

There are certain moments in life that don't feel like endings or beginnings while you're in them. They just feel like survival. You don't have the distance yet to understand what's happening, and you don't have the language yet to explain it. You're simply moving from one hour to the next, trying to hold yourself together in ways nobody else can see. That's what the days after Ohio State felt like. Not fixed. Not resolved. Not even clearly improving. Just different in a way I didn't yet know how to interpret.

During my Ohio State four-week program that was recommended that I partake in, I still struggled to understand, even when the facts, evidence, and results were sitting right in front of me. I did a lot during my time there. There were group-therapy sessions, individual reflection, and lectures/workshops. We focused on a plethora of notions—self-compassion, grief, unhealthy relationships, and my favorite: early maladaptive schemas. I was so intrigued and involved that I created a test that anyone can confidentially take and get feedback based on your input—mhlib.netlify.app.

I remember thinking a lot about control during that time. Or maybe more accurately, the loss of it. Before all of this, I believed I had a stronger grip on my thoughts than I actually did. I thought if something felt wrong, I could reason my way out of it. If something scared me, I could think through it until it made sense again. But anxiety doesn't always respond to logic. In fact, it often grows louder when you try to argue with it. The more I tried to convince myself I was okay, the more my mind seemed to search for evidence that I wasn't. It became a cycle I didn't know how to break. Fear created the thought, the thought created the feeling, and the feeling confirmed the fear.

What I didn't understand yet was that recovery wasn't going to come from out-thinking my own mind. It was going to come from learning how to exist alongside it again. That idea would have confused me at the time. Existing alongside my own mind already felt like the problem. I didn't want to coexist with fear. I wanted it gone. I wanted silence. I wanted the version of myself that didn't constantly analyze every sensation, every thought, every moment of awareness. But silence wasn't something I could force. Every attempt to force it only made the noise louder.

There were days when I would feel almost normal for a few hours, and I would mistake that for progress. Then, without warning, the fear would return, and it would feel even heavier than before. That unpredictability wore me down more than anything else. I never knew which version of myself I was going to wake up as. Some mornings I felt slightly connected. Other mornings I felt distant again, like I was watching my own life through something I couldn't touch. It made trusting my own experience incredibly difficult because my experience kept changing without warning.

Still, something was slowly shifting, even if I couldn't see it clearly at the time. I was beginning to learn that not every thought deserved my full attention. Not every feeling required investigation. Not every moment of discomfort was a sign that something was wrong. Those realizations didn't arrive all at once. They came in fragments, often after long stretches of fear. Sometimes I would realize, after hours of spiraling, that nothing had actually changed except my reaction to my thoughts. Other times I would catch myself stepping back from fear just slightly sooner than before. It wasn't dramatic. It wasn't clean. But it was movement.

And movement mattered.

Because for a long time, I had felt completely stuck inside my own mind. Like I was standing in the same place mentally, no matter how much time passed. The idea that I might actually be shifting, even slowly, even imperfectly, was something I didn't fully believe yet—but I was starting to notice it.

The truth is, I didn't have a clear turning point. There wasn't a single moment where everything changed. There wasn't a sentence that fixed it. There wasn't a realization that ended the fear. What there were, instead, were small interruptions in the cycle. Small pauses in the panic. Small moments where I realized I had made it through something I thought I wouldn't. Those moments didn't feel powerful at the time, but they added up in ways I couldn't see yet.

And maybe that's the part I needed most back then. Not certainty. Not answers. Not control.

Just proof, over and over again, that I was still here.

Still thinking.

Still moving.

Still me, even when I didn't feel like it.

And even though I didn't understand it yet, that was enough to begin with.

There are things I wish I could say I understood in that moment. I wish I could say I knew I was going to be okay. I wish I could say I felt strong, or grounded, or even remotely certain about what came next. But the truth is that I didn't feel any of those things. I was still scared. Still uncertain. Still trying to understand what had just happened inside my own mind. And even though the worst of the episode had passed, nothing inside me felt settled.

What I remember most about that time isn't clarity. It's endurance. It's waking up each day not knowing exactly what version of myself I am going to get, but getting up anyway. It's sitting in classrooms while feeling like I was slightly detached from everything around me. It's having conversations and responding at the right times while quietly wondering if anyone else could tell that something inside me had changed. On the surface, life kept moving the same way it always had. Beneath it, everything felt unfamiliar.

I used to think the hard part would be the moment everything broke. That there would be a single point where things reached their worst and then immediately began to heal. But that's not how it happened. There was no clean breaking point and no clean recovery. Instead, there was something in between. A space I didn't have a name for yet. A space where I was no longer in the middle of the crisis, but I also wasn't free from it. I just existed inside it.

There were still moments of fear. Still moments where my thoughts didn't feel fully mine. Still moments where I questioned whether I was okay or whether I ever would be again. But those moments started to stretch out differently. Sometimes I would go longer without spiraling. Sometimes I would catch myself before fear fully took over. Sometimes I would realize, briefly, that I had made it through a part of the day without analyzing every sensation in my mind. None of it felt like progress at the time. It just felt like survival continuing in a slightly different form.

And maybe that's why I didn't notice the shift happening.

Because it wasn't dramatic.

It didn't announce itself.

It didn't feel like healing.

It felt like confusion that lasted just a little less intensely than before.

Still, something was changing, even if I didn't have the language for it yet. I was beginning to live inside a version of life where fear didn't disappear, but it also didn't define every moment the way it once had. I didn't understand that this mattered yet. I didn't understand that I was slowly learning how to stay present even when my mind wasn't cooperating. I didn't understand that I was already moving forward, even while it still felt like I was stuck.

All I knew was that I was still here.

Still thinking.

Still trying.

And still living inside a mind I no longer fully trusted, waiting for something I couldn't name yet to change.

And I didn't know it at the time, but the next chapter of my life wasn't going to be about what happened to me anymore.

It was going to be about what happened after I started living inside it.

3

Living Behind Glass

The first thing I learned was that calm doesn't always feel like calm.

There's a strange space that opens up after the loudest moments are over, when nothing inside you has fully returned to normal but the world has already decided you're fine. On the outside, life moves on immediately. School continues. Conversations continue. Expectations don't pause just because your mind has been through something you don't know how to explain. People assume that if you're no longer visibly falling apart, you must be okay again.

I wasn't okay again. I was something there isn't a clean word for.

In the first chapter of this book, I wrote about a boy who trusted his mind without ever realizing it was something that could be trusted or not. For thirteen years, my mind was simply home. I didn't study it. I didn't monitor it. I didn't wake up and check whether it still worked. It was just the place I lived from, the way you live in a house without thinking about the foundation underneath it. I wrote that I assumed reality would always feel real, that my thoughts would always feel familiar, that my mind would always be a place I could trust.

This is the chapter where I have to tell you what it's like once that's gone.

Because after April 17th, after the weekend that split my life into before and after, I didn't get to go back to being that boy. I had stepped out of a burning room and into a hallway where I could still smell the smoke. My body was no longer in full alarm, but my mind hadn't stopped scanning for danger. And without deciding to, I had started living one step removed from my own life—watching it happen instead of being inside it, like there was a pane of glass between me and everything else.

That's the closest way I can describe it.

Like living behind glass.

What made it so disorienting is that it didn't show. Everything looked normal. School looked normal. Conversations looked normal. Even moments of laughter still happened. But I didn't feel fully inside any of it. I could understand what someone was saying to me and, at the same time, feel slightly removed from the fact that they were saying it. I could respond at the right moment, in the right tone, while part of my mind ran its quiet background questions. Do I feel real right now? Does this feel normal? Am I okay yet? I never chose to ask them. They just ran, like something my brain had learned to keep on at all times.

I keep coming back to the boy from the first chapter, because the comparison is almost cruel. That kid loved school. I wrote that he loved having somewhere to be every day, loved having a purpose, loved the routine of it. I said that school gave him something he wouldn't fully appreciate until years later—it occupied his mind. His thoughts weren't his focus. Life was.

Now life was the thing happening on the other side of the glass, and my thoughts were the only thing I could focus on.

I want to be honest about where this lived, because people always want to know the specifics. They ask if it was worse in certain places. Was it the big lecture halls? The crowded hallways? Tests? And I understand the question, because most struggles have a location. Most fears have a room you can avoid. But that's not how this worked for me, and I think the truth is more important than a tidy answer.

It was everywhere. All the time. Every day, every time.

It didn't matter if I was in a lecture hall or walking across campus or sitting in my own room afterward. It didn't matter if I was in class or out of it, busy or still, alone or surrounded by people. There was no setting where the glass lifted. There was no room I could walk into and finally feel like myself again. I couldn't escape it by changing where I was, because the thing I needed to escape was coming with me. It was me, or at least it was wearing me, and you can't leave a place you're carrying.

That's the part I couldn't make anyone understand at first. People imagine you get breaks. They picture you struggling in one moment and relieved in the next, the way ordinary stress comes and goes. But this didn't come and go. It was the baseline. It was the weather I lived in. Even in moments that should have been easy—sitting with friends, laughing at something, eating a meal—there was a second version of me standing just behind the first one, checking. Are you here for this? Do you feel this? Is this real?

And because I never stopped functioning, part of me kept

insisting I must be fine—which didn't bring relief, only another layer of confusion. How could I be struggling this much on the inside and look this normal on the outside? What did it mean that I could do both at once?

I wrote in the second chapter that a person can be drowning and still appear calm from the shore. I knew that was true because I was doing it. I was drowning in a way that didn't make a sound. From across a room, you would have seen a young man going to class, answering questions, showing up. You would not have seen the glass. You would not have seen the second version of me, the one keeping watch.

People did notice something, occasionally. Not the real thing—they could never see the real thing—but a flicker of it. A quietness where there used to be more of me. A delay before I answered. And every so often, someone would ask.

"You good?"

"You okay?"

It always landed harder than they meant it to. A simple, throwaway question, the kind people ask each other a hundred times a day without thinking. But every time someone asked, I felt the floor tilt a little, because for one second I thought maybe it was showing. Maybe the glass was visible after all. Maybe they could see that I wasn't fully there.

And so I learned to perform the answer.

"Yeah, I'm fine. Why?"

That was the line. I said it more times than I could count, and the most important part of it was the why at the end. The why did the work. It turned the question around. It put the strangeness back on them, made it sound like they were the ones imagining things, made it impossible for them to keep looking too closely without feeling like they were the ones being weird. Why? As if I had no idea what they could possibly be picking up on. As if there were nothing there to pick up on at all.

It worked every time. That was the worst part. It always worked. People would shrug and say no reason, you just seemed quiet, and the conversation would move on, and I would be left standing exactly where I'd been—behind the glass, alone with it, having just successfully convinced one more person that there was nothing to see.

I got good at it. Frighteningly good. I could hold a normal face. I could nod at the right times. I could laugh on cue, half a second after everyone else, close enough that no one noticed the delay. I could carry an entire conversation while monitoring whether I felt present enough to be having it. The performance became so automatic that sometimes I'd realize I'd gotten through a whole interaction on autopilot, having said all the right things, without ever having actually been there for any of it.

The boy in the first chapter never performed anything. I wrote that he always had something to say, that quiet was never his natural state, that if there was a conversation happening he wanted to join it and if there was a game being played he wanted in. He threw himself into things completely because he was fully present in his life. He wasn't standing on the sidelines watching it happen. He was in it.

I had become someone who was only ever on the sidelines, watching it happen, while pretending to be in it.

There was exactly one person I didn't fully perform for. My mom.

She was the one place the glass could thin a little, the one person I could be even partly honest with. But honesty has its own problem, which is that this thing is almost impossible to put into words. I would try to describe it and hear how small it sounded out loud. I don't feel real. I feel like I'm watching my own life. It never came out the size it actually was. The words were too light for the weight they were supposed to carry.

The first time I really tried, she was out of town.

I texted her. I told her what had happened—the panic attack, the thing that had cracked everything open—and I told her something was wrong. Not ordinary wrong. Seriously wrong. I told her I had moved my doctor's appointment up so I could be seen sooner, because I didn't feel alive. Because I didn't feel real. I remember trying to make her understand that this wasn't me being dramatic or stressed about school, that this was something I had never felt before and couldn't switch off.

And she tried. She really did. She tried to relate to it, tried to connect it to something she understood, tried to meet me where I was. I know now that she was doing the most loving thing she knew how to do. But in that moment, being related to made me feel more alone, not less. Because what I was describing didn't have a comparison. There was nothing to relate it to. Every time she reached for something familiar to hold it next to, I felt the distance between what I was living and what she could picture, and that distance made me feel unheard in a way I didn't have the energy to fix over text.

That's one of the loneliest parts of this whole thing. Even the people who love you most, even the people doing everything right, can't always reach you, because the place you're calling from doesn't have an address they've ever been to.

What changed wasn't a conversation. It was a moment she actually saw.

We were sitting on the couch together. My feet were in her lap. It was an ordinary, domestic, safe arrangement—the kind of closeness that has existed between us my whole life. In the first chapter I wrote about sitting at a tiny table during a tea party with her, both of us drinking lemon tea out of teacups, and how that was the most important thing in the world. Same mom. Same lap, almost. Years apart.

And then a panic attack came, right there, with no warning and nowhere to hide it.

I couldn't perform through that one. There was no "yeah, I'm fine, why." There was just it, happening to me, in front of her, while my feet were in her lap and there was nothing either of us could do to stop it. And I watched her face change. I watched something land in her that hadn't landed over text, no matter what I'd said. She got serious in a way she hadn't been able to before—not because she hadn't believed me, but because now she could see it. Now it wasn't words too light for their weight. It was right there in the room with both of us.

I don't know how to explain what it meant to be believed like that. To not have to convince someone. To not have to turn the question around with a why. For one terrible, honest moment, the glass wasn't between me and the person I loved, because she was finally seeing the same thing I was seeing.

It didn't fix anything. I want to be clear about that, because this isn't the chapter where things get better. The panic still happened. The glass was still there the next morning. I still had to get up and go to class and say I was fine and mean none of it. But something was different in knowing that at least one person knew the real version, that I didn't have to carry the entire performance alone everywhere, forever.

Still, most of it I did carry alone. That's just the truth of it. A few people knew a little. One person had seen the worst. But the day-to-day reality—the every-day, every-time, everywhere of it—was mine to move through, mostly in silence, mostly behind the glass, mostly while telling the world I was fine and asking why anyone would think otherwise.

The hardest question in those days wasn't whether it would ever end. It was simpler and worse than that. I couldn't tell whether I was getting better or just getting used to it. I would have a stretch of hours where I felt a little more solid, and I wouldn't trust it. I would have a stretch where I felt far away again, and I'd assume that was the real truth and the good hours had been a fluke. My own sense of how I was doing became unreliable, which meant I couldn't even use myself as a measure anymore.

So I kept showing up. I sat in classrooms and listened to lessons while carrying an entire internal world no one could see. I completed the assignments. I made it to the next thing, and the next. I said "yeah, I'm fine, why" to everyone who asked, and I saved the truth for the one couch where someone had finally seen it.

In the first chapter, I wrote that what I missed most about the person I used to be wasn't that he was happier. Life wasn't perfect then either. What I missed was the certainty. I trusted my mind. I trusted reality. I trusted that the world around me was exactly what it appeared to be.

Now I trusted none of it, and I was being asked to live a completely normal life on top of that mistrust, every single day, without letting it show.

From the outside it looked like a young man going to college.

From the inside it was the most tiring thing I have ever

done.

4

The Weight of the Storm

There's a moment after everything loud goes quiet when you expect relief to arrive immediately, like it's been waiting just outside the door the whole time.

I thought that once the worst of it passed, I would finally feel like myself again. I thought I'd wake up one morning and recognize myself instantly, as if nothing had happened. What I found instead was quieter, and in some ways harder to understand.

Because silence doesn't feel like peace when you've spent a long time living in noise.

I'm not going to walk you back through the night of April 17th in detail. I wrote about it earlier, and some things don't get clearer by being told twice. But I'll say this much, because this chapter doesn't make sense without it: I was at home, lying on my back in bed, and it came out of nowhere. There was no warning. No buildup I could point to. No bad day that explained it. One moment I was a person lying in bed, and the next moment something arrived that I had no name for and no defense against, and by the time it passed, the line between before and after had already been drawn behind me.

That was the storm.

This chapter is about what it left.

Because here's what nobody tells you about a storm like that. You brace for the storm itself. You assume that the loud part, the terrifying part, the part where it feels like you're being torn out of your own life, is the worst it gets. And then the loud part ends, and you discover that the quiet it leaves behind is its own kind of hard. The wind stops. The noise stops. And you're left standing in the wreckage, too hollowed-out to feel relieved, wondering why the ending doesn't feel like an ending.

At first I didn't even register that anything had changed in me. Life kept going the way it always had—class, conversations, routines, the small responsibilities that don't wait for you to feel ready. On the outside nothing looked different. On the inside, I was adjusting to the absence of something that had taken up enormous space, and I didn't have anything to put in its place.

The word for what I felt is numb. Not calm. Not better. Numb.

I keep reaching for ways to describe it, and the closest I can get is that it felt like the volume on everything had been turned down—not just the bad things, but all of it. Color, interest, the ordinary pull of being alive. In the first chapter, I wrote about a boy who threw himself into everything completely. Who hated losing because he cared. Who turned roads into racetracks and patches of woods into unexplored territory, for whom every day held the possibility of an adventure. I wrote that he was fully present in his life, that he wasn't standing on the sidelines watching it happen. He was in it.

The person lying in the wreckage of that storm couldn't feel any of that anymore. Not the caring. Not the wanting. Not the pull. Things that should have moved me didn't move me. Things that should have mattered slid past like they were happening behind glass to someone else. I wasn't sad, exactly. Sad would have been something. I was flat. I was running on a kind of emotional silence that I couldn't switch back off, and the strangest part was that from the outside, flat can look a lot like fine.

But underneath the numbness there was always one thing still running, and it never stopped.

I was waiting for it to come back.

That's the part I most need you to understand about the after. Even in the numbness, even on the days that looked calm, part of me stayed braced. Always. Because I had learned, on April 17th, that it could arrive out of nowhere—that there didn't have to be a reason, didn't have to be a warning, didn't have to be a bad day leading up to it. It had come for me while I was just lying in bed. And once you learn that, you can never fully relax again, because the lesson your body takes from it is that nowhere is safe and no moment is exempt. If it could come from nothing, it could come from anything. So I waited. Lying in bed at night, I waited. Sitting in a quiet moment that should have been peaceful, I waited. The calm itself became a thing I couldn't trust, because the last time things were calm, I was lying on my back in bed, and then I wasn't okay anymore.

When you live braced like that, calm stops meaning "nothing is wrong." It starts meaning "it hasn't happened yet."

And then there's the part that's hardest to admit, the part I almost left out of this book because I was afraid of how it would sound.

A little piece of me missed the fear.

Not the suffering. I want to be careful here, because I'm not saying I missed being afraid. I'm saying that fear, for all its horror, at least had a shape. It told me what to do with my attention. It gave the day a center. When you're terrified, you at least know you're alive, because terror is a loud, undeniable signal that something inside you is still firing. The numbness didn't even give me that. The numbness was a kind of nothing, and there were moments—quiet, ashamed moments I never said out loud to anyone—where the nothing felt worse than the fear had, because at least the fear had been proof that I was still in there somewhere.

It's a strange thing to miss something that hurt you, only because you knew its shape.

I think this is one of the loneliest stretches of the whole experience, and it's the one people understand least. Everyone gets the loud part. Everyone can picture panic, fear, a crisis. What they can't picture is the after—the long, gray, numb stretch where the emergency is technically over but you don't feel saved, just emptied. There's a grief in it I didn't have a name for at the time. You expect the end of the worst part to feel like winning. Instead it feels like standing in a room after everyone's gone home, surrounded by the mess, too tired to clean it up and too numb to care that it's there.

In the first chapter, I wrote about the feeling I missed most from before all of this. Not happiness—I was careful to say it wasn't happiness, because life before wasn't perfect either. What I missed was the certainty. The feeling that tomorrow would arrive looking more or less like today. I trusted that the world around me was exactly what it appeared to be.

The storm took that, and what it left in its place was the

opposite of certainty. It left a permanent sense that tomorrow might not look like today at all—that today might not even make it to tonight intact. The boy from the first chapter assumed reality would always feel real. The person in the wreckage assumed nothing, braced for everything, and felt almost none of it.

I want to be honest that I didn't resolve any of this by understanding it. At this point in the story, I didn't have it figured out. I'm not even sure I have it fully figured out now. I only had the deflating discovery that surviving the loudest part of something is not the same as being free of it, and that nobody had warned me there would be an after that felt like this. An after that was quiet, and heavy, and lonelier in its own way than the noise had been.

The hardest thing to accept was that it didn't lift. I kept waiting for the numbness to break, the way I'd waited for the fear to come back—as if eventually I'd wake up and the weight would just be gone. It didn't work like that. It never fully lifted. It thinned in places, over a long time, in ways I'll get to later in this book. But that clean morning where I woke up and the storm had simply passed and the sky was blue again? It never came. I had to learn to live with weather that doesn't end.

That was the weight of the storm. Not the storm itself.

What it left in me once it moved on.

And the fact that it didn't really move on at all—it just changed from something loud into something I carry.

5

The Watching Mind

I want to slow down here and describe the actual machine of it, because for a long time I didn't understand that the thing making everything worse was the thing I was using to try to make it better.

This is the chapter I almost didn't know how to write, because what I'm about to describe is the part that sounds the most alarming from the outside and felt the most logical from the inside. That's the trap of it. While you're in it, none of it feels irrational. Every piece of it feels like the only reasonable response to what's happening to you. It's only later, looking back, that you can see the whole shape of the machine and understand that you were the one feeding it.

So let me start with the machine itself.

Somewhere in all of this, my mind developed a habit of checking itself. Constantly. Not on purpose—it had simply learned that safety depended on never fully looking away from itself, so it didn't. There was no off switch. I don't mean that as a figure of speech. I mean there was no moment, waking, when some part of my attention wasn't turned inward, running its inspection. The second I woke up, before I'd even gotten out of bed, it started. How do I feel? Do I feel real? Is anything off? I ran my attention over my own mind the way you'd run a hand along a wall in the dark, feeling for the thing that wasn't right. And it never stopped. It ran while I was in class. It ran while I was talking to people. It ran while I was trying to fall asleep, which is its own special cruelty, because the one thing that's supposed to give you a break from your mind is sleep, and I couldn't get there because my mind wouldn't stop checking whether it was okay enough to rest.

Here is the cruelest part of the mechanics, the part I wish someone had explained to me sooner. The more I checked for the feeling of being okay, the harder it became to find.

Being okay isn't something you can hold still and examine. It's something you only have when you're not looking at it. Think about walking. You can walk across a room without a single thought, smoothly, automatically—until someone asks you to pay attention to exactly how you're moving your legs, and suddenly the walking goes stiff and strange and you nearly trip over a process you've done ten thousand times. That's what I had done to my entire experience of being alive. I had turned the floodlight of my attention onto processes that are only supposed to run in the dark. Feeling real. Feeling present. Feeling like myself. The moment I looked directly at any of them to check if they were working, they stopped feeling like they were working, because attention is the one thing they can't survive. It was like trying to stare directly at something that only exists in the corner of your eye. The act of searching for it was what made it disappear.

So I'd check, and the checking would make me feel worse,

and feeling worse would convince me I needed to check more, and checking more would make me feel worse still. That was the loop. Around and around, all day, every day, with no exit that I could find, because every tool I had for finding an exit was the same tool that was digging the hole deeper.

And the checking didn't stay in my head. It took physical forms, and this is where it gets harder to explain to someone who hasn't lived it, so I'm going to try to be as plain as I can.

I touched things. Constantly. I would put my hand on a desk, a wall, a table, whatever was near me, just to confirm it was solid, that it was there, that I was there among real things. I would stare at my own hands, turning them over, trying to feel that they were mine and not just shapes I was looking at. And then it went somewhere stranger. I started checking for shadows. I would look at an object, or at a person, and I would look for the shadow it cast, because a shadow meant the thing was physically there, occupying space, blocking light—and if I could confirm the shadow, maybe I could believe the thing was real.

I did this with people. I want to say that part out loud because it's the part that scared me most. I would be looking at a real person, someone right in front of me, and some part of my mind would be checking them for their shadow to confirm they actually existed. Because I had started assuming that everything might be a hallucination. Not because I was actually hallucinating—I want to be clear about that—but because I had become so unsure of my own perception that I treated reality as guilty until proven innocent. Presumptive hallucinations, where the default assumption became this isn't real until I could find some piece of evidence to argue myself out of it.

Live like that long enough and it poisons everything.

Because once you genuinely aren't sure whether anything around you is real, a terrible logic starts to build, and it builds quietly, and it makes a horrible kind of sense from the inside. If the conversation I'm having might not be real, then why am I putting energy into it? If the person in front of me might not be real, what's the point of connecting with them? If none of this is real, why do anything at all? Why try in school, why show up, why care about any of it, when I can't even confirm that the world I'd be doing it for exists? I remember the thought arriving fully formed: nothing else matters, so why give it my energy. I should just do whatever I want, because none of it counts anyway.

That's one of the loneliest places this whole thing took me. It cut me off from people not because I didn't want them, but because I couldn't trust that they were there. It drained the meaning out of effort, out of conversation, out of the ordinary business of being a person, because meaning requires believing that the thing you're investing in is real, and I had lost the ability to believe that.

And on top of all of it sat the fear. The constant, grinding fear that this was it now. That I was losing my mind in a permanent way. That this wasn't a phase or a symptom or a state that would pass, but the new shape of my life forever. I was exhausted by it in a way that sleep couldn't touch, and I was convinced—genuinely convinced—that it was never going to end.

I want to stop here and put this next to the boy from the first chapter, because the distance is almost unbearable to look at directly.

That boy trusted reality without ever once thinking about it.

I wrote that he never worried about whether he felt connected to his surroundings, never questioned whether he felt real, that the idea itself would have sounded absurd to him. His mind wasn't something he studied or analyzed. It was simply home. He assumed reality would always feel real. He assumed his thoughts would always feel familiar. He assumed his mind would always be a place he could trust.

And here was the same person, years later, checking strangers for their shadows to confirm they existed. Assuming the world was a hallucination until proven otherwise. Wondering why he should bother talking to anyone, since he couldn't be sure they were there. The boy who turned woods into unexplored territory and roads into racetracks, who threw himself into everything because he was so completely, unquestioningly inside his own life—that same boy, now standing one full step outside reality, knocking on the glass, asking it to prove it was real.

That's what I need you to understand before the next part makes any sense. The loop wasn't a side effect of the problem. The loop was the problem. The watching wasn't how I was coping. The watching had become the thing I needed to be saved from, and it had disguised itself as the search for safety so completely that I couldn't see it.

So how does anyone get out of a trap like that?

I'll tell you how it started for me, and I'll warn you ahead of time that it isn't inspiring. It isn't a breakthrough. There was no moment of clarity, no wise words from anyone, no morning where I woke up and understood. The first time I managed not to chase the feeling, it wasn't because I was strong.

It was because I was too tired to fight it anymore.

That's the honest truth, and I've decided to keep it honest in this book even though a better story would have a braver turning point. There wasn't one. There was just a day, one of countless identical days inside the loop, where the feeling came—that wave of unreality, that pull to start checking, to touch something, to find a shadow, to run the inspection one more time—and I just… didn't. Not because I'd decided not to. Not because I'd learned some technique. I didn't have it in me anymore. I had run completely out of the energy it takes to chase your own reality around in circles all day, and so for once, I let the feeling sit there without doing anything about it.

I want to describe what that was like, because it's so much smaller and stranger than people imagine recovery looking.

It wasn't peaceful. It wasn't a relief. It was more like collapsing than like choosing. The feeling was still there—the distance, the unreality, the wrongness—and I was just lying underneath it, too depleted to argue with it, letting it be there because fighting it cost more than I had left. And in that exhausted surrender, with my guard finally down because I literally couldn't hold it up anymore, something happened that I wasn't expecting.

Nothing.

Nothing happened.

The feeling came, and I didn't chase it, and the thing I had spent all that energy trying to prevent simply didn't occur. I didn't lose my mind. I didn't slip away. The unreality didn't swallow me whole the way I'd always believed it would if I ever stopped fighting it. It just sat there for a while, and then—without my doing anything, without a single check or touch or shadow—it loosened on its own. It passed. Or it faded. Or it just stopped being the only thing in the room. I honestly couldn't tell you the mechanics of it, only that the catastrophe I'd been bracing against, the one I'd been running from with every checking ritual I had, never came. And I had done nothing to stop it. That was the impossible part. I had done nothing, and nothing bad had happened.

I'd love to tell you that I understood the significance of it right away. I didn't. The first few times it happened, I think I assumed I'd just gotten lucky, or that it didn't count, or that it would be different next time. But it kept happening. The pattern, very slowly, became impossible to ignore: the times I was too tired to fight the feeling were not the times it got worse. Sometimes they were the times it passed soonest. The feeling I had treated as a five-alarm fire for months turned out, when I stopped pouring fuel on it, to often just burn down to nothing by itself.

That was the discovery the whole rest of my story rests on. The feeling had never been the danger. My reaction to it was what gave it its size.

And here is where I have to be careful, because this is the exact point where books like this usually lie to you, and I don't want to.

Learning this did not make the feeling go away. I want to say that as plainly as I can. I did not discover a trick that ended my struggle. To this day I have not made the feeling stop, and I have stopped expecting to. What I found in that exhausted surrender wasn't an off switch. It was something quieter and, in the long run, more useful: a gap.

A small space between the feeling and my reaction to it.

Before, there was no gap. The feeling arrived and I was already gone—already checking, already touching, already hunting for shadows, already deep in the loop before I'd even registered that it had started. Feeling and reaction were a single motion, instant, automatic, like a reflex I couldn't interrupt. What being too tired to fight gave me, by accident, was the first time those two things came apart. The feeling, over here. My reaction to it, over there. And in between them, for the first time, a sliver of space where I got to do something other than run.

I didn't always use that space well. For a long time I'd notice the feeling, find the gap, and still get pulled all the way into the loop anyway, just a half-second slower than before. But the gap was there now, and it hadn't been before, and once you know a gap exists you can't fully unknow it. You start, very clumsily, very inconsistently, to step into it on purpose. To feel the wave of unreality arrive and not immediately touch the desk. To catch myself reaching to check a shadow and, sometimes, let my hand stay still. To notice the old logic starting up—this might not be real, so why bother—and not follow it all the way down to its terrible conclusion.

Not every time. I want to keep being honest. Plenty of times the loop still won. But there were now days, scattered and unreliable at first, where it didn't. Where I felt the whole machine start up and I just... let it run without me. Where I learned, against everything my fear had taught me, that I did not have to chase the feeling to be safe from it. That the chasing had never been keeping me safe in the first place. That it had been the loop all along.

And that pause—that small, exhausted, accidental space between the feeling and the reaction—changed everything.

Not because it made me okay. I want to end this chapter on the truth rather than the comfort. It didn't make me okay.

It gave me something better suited to a struggle that doesn't end: a moment, in the middle of the worst of it, where I didn't have to run.

That moment was the beginning of everything that came after.

It just didn't feel like a beginning at the time.

It felt like giving up.

And the strangest lesson of my entire life is that, that one time, giving up the fight was the closest thing to winning I had found.

6

The Quiet Between

I don't think I'll ever fully stop noticing my own mind.

I want to start there, honestly, because this is the chapter where things get quieter, and I don't want "quieter" to be mistaken for "over." Even as things have improved in small ways, even as the worst moments have come less often, there is a level of awareness in me now that wasn't there before any of this started. Something in me learned how to monitor itself, and that part doesn't just leave. It quiets down. It loosens its grip. But it stays in the background of how I experience everything, like a sound you've gotten used to but can still hear if you stop and listen for it.

I've had to learn not to be afraid of that fact. And I want to be clear about where I'm writing this from, because I think the honest version is more useful to you than the tidy one.

I am not on the other side of this.

I'm somewhere in the middle of it, in a place that doesn't have a clean name. Not the crisis. Not recovered. The quiet in between. And that in-between is where I actually live now, so it's the place I most want to describe, because nobody warned me it existed, and I think it would have helped to know it was coming. When you're in the loudest part of something like this, you imagine there are only two possible destinations: the nightmare you're living, or the old life you lost. You don't realize there's a third place. A long, quiet hallway between the two, where you spend far more time than anyone tells you about. That hallway is where I live now. This chapter is a map of it.

Let me tell you what it looks like day to day, because the day to day is the whole truth of it.

The numbness still shows up. The detachment still shows up. The feeling that things are slightly unreal, that I'm watching instead of living, that there's a thin distance between me and the moment I'm in—that part hasn't disappeared. It visits most days, in some size. I want to say that plainly, because if you're in the worst of it right now and someone tells you they're "better," I think you deserve to know exactly what better has meant for me. It hasn't meant the feeling left. It has meant the feeling got quieter, and I got bigger around it.

If I'm describing a normal day now, here's the honest shape of it: I manage it, quietly, all day. That's the phrase that fits best. I don't wake up cured. I wake up and the feeling is often already there, a low background hum of unreality, and I get up and go about my day anyway while quietly managing it underneath everything else. I go to my classes. I talk to people. I do the things a person my age does. And the whole time, in the background, I'm carrying it—not fighting it the way I used to, not running checks all day the way I used to, but aware of it, managing it, living alongside it. From the outside, you would not be able to tell. That part hasn't changed since the early chapters. What's changed is what's happening on the inside while I look fine on the outside. Before, the inside was a war. Now the inside is more like maintenance. Quiet, constant, manageable maintenance.

That might not sound like much of a victory. I understand that. "I manage it quietly all day" is not the triumphant recovery story people want to hear. But I need you to understand the distance between that and where I was, because measured against the chapters that came before, it's enormous. There was a time when I couldn't manage it at all—when it managed me, when it took the whole day, when it took the whole room. The fact that I can now carry it quietly in the background while living an actual life is not a small thing. It's the thing. It's most of what recovery has actually meant for me.

The feeling didn't shrink so much as everything else in me grew back enough to hold it. There was a time when the unreality was the entire room—when it took up all of me, all of my attention, all of my fear, with no space left over for anything else. Now it's one thing in a larger room. It's still there. I can still feel it. But it isn't the only furniture anymore. There's other stuff in the room now. Some of it is even good.

The thing that changed most isn't the presence of the feeling. It's the meaning I attach to it.

There was a time when any shift inside me was an alarm. One uncomfortable sensation meant everything—it could take over my focus, my sense of safety, my sense of what was real, and stretch out into hours or days where I couldn't separate what I was feeling from what I believed was happening. One sensation meant everything. One thought meant everything. One moment meant everything. Every flicker of unreality was treated as breaking news, a five-alarm fire, proof that the collapse I'd been dreading was finally arriving.

Now it doesn't always expand like that. Sometimes the feeling stays small. Sometimes it passes. Sometimes I move through it and only realize afterward that it came and went without swallowing the day. And I've had to learn to count that as something real, even when it doesn't feel dramatic enough to look like progress in the moment. Because that's what progress has actually been for me—not a finish line, not a cure, but a quieter relationship with the same noise. The volume coming down. The fire becoming a flicker. The flicker becoming something I can have in the room without dropping everything to put it out.

I owe a lot of that to getting help, and I want to talk about that honestly, because I spent a long time before I did.

For most of the worst of it, I tried to carry the whole thing inside my own head—the same head that was lying to me about what was real. Looking back, that's almost funny in a dark way. I was using the broken instrument to try to fix the broken instrument. I was asking the mind that had convinced me nothing was real to also be the thing that talked me back down. It couldn't. Of course it couldn't. It was too far inside the loop to see the loop. You cannot think your way out of a problem when thinking is the thing that's malfunctioning. It's like trying to read the label from inside the bottle.

What helped was getting outside of my own head. A doctor. A therapist. Someone whose entire job was to look at what I was describing from the outside, from a place I couldn't stand on anymore.

And what they did for me wasn't a magic technique. I think

people expect therapy to be a set of clever tricks, and maybe sometimes it is, but that's not what mattered most for me. What mattered most was almost embarrassingly simple.

They believed me.

That's it. That's the thing that started to turn the lights back on. For so long I had been describing something that sounded insane even to me, something I could barely put into words, something that made the people who loved me reach for comparisons that didn't quite fit and left me feeling more alone than before I'd opened my mouth. I wrote earlier about texting my mom, about how she tried to relate and how being related to somehow made me feel more unheard, because what I was living didn't have a comparison. And then I sat across from someone who didn't flinch, didn't reach for a comparison, didn't try to relate it to a bad week they'd once had. They just heard it. They recognized it. They had a name for it, and the name meant other people had felt this too, which meant I wasn't the first human being to fall out of reality and I wouldn't be the last.

That alone—just being recognized—did something no amount of self-reassurance had managed. Because part of the terror had always been the loneliness of it, the sense that I was the only person this had ever happened to, that I had invented a brand-new way to be broken. To find out it had a name was to find out it had a shape, and a shape is something that can be understood, mapped, and survived. Things with names have been survived by other people. Things with names are not the end of the world. They just feel like it.

And then they told me the two things my own mind had spent months insisting were false.

It isn't dangerous.

It isn't permanent.

I need you to understand what it was like to hear those words, because by that point my mind had built an entire world on the opposite of them. My whole internal reality was constructed on two certainties: that this was dangerous—that I was losing my mind, that I might never come back, that I was actively in the process of breaking—and that it was permanent—that this was simply my life now, forever, with no exit. Those two beliefs were the walls of the prison. Everything I felt got interpreted through them. And here was someone who knew more about this than I did, who had seen it many times in many people, calmly telling me that both walls were false.

I'd love to tell you I felt relief. I didn't. Not at first.

At first, I didn't believe them.

That's the honest reaction, and I'm keeping it in the book, because I think it's important for anyone in the same place to know that disbelief is normal and isn't a sign you're the exception. When someone tells you the thing you've been certain of is wrong, you don't just drop the certainty because they said so. The certainty had been with me every hour of every day. It had been confirmed, in my mind, thousands of times by thousands of checks. A few sentences from a professional, no matter how qualified, couldn't undo all of that in an afternoon. Part of me sat there thinking, you don't understand, mine is different, mine is the real thing, mine is the one that doesn't get better, mine is the one you've never actually seen before. The disbelief was its own symptom. The illness was arguing for its own permanence, the way it always had. That's what these things do. They convince you that they're the exception to every reassurance, including the reassurance that they're not the exception.

But here's what was different this time, and why it mattered even though I didn't believe it yet. I now had something I hadn't had before: another voice. Someone outside the loop, saying the opposite of what the loop was saying. And I could hold those two things next to each other—the loop insisting it was permanent and dangerous, and a real human being who'd seen this many times insisting it was neither—and for the first time, there was a contest. Before, the loop had run completely unopposed. It was the only voice in the room, and a voice with no opposition becomes the truth by default. Now there was a second opinion in the room, and even if I couldn't fully trust it yet, its mere existence cracked the certainty. And a certainty with a crack in it is no longer a certainty. It's just a very loud opinion. That crack was the beginning of everything.

Because slowly—slowly—the evidence started coming in on the side of the people who told me it wasn't permanent.

It did keep changing. Not in a straight line. Not into a cure. But the quieter days started, very gradually, to outnumber the loudest ones. The feeling kept proving, over and over, that it could pass—that it had passed, again and again, every single time so far, no matter how convinced I'd been in the moment that this time it wouldn't. I was building, without meaning to, a pile of evidence that the catastrophe never actually arrived. Every time I survived a wave I'd been sure would end me, another piece went on the pile. And eventually the pile got tall enough that I had to start believing what they'd told me—not because I decided to, but because the facts of my own life kept voting for it, day after day, until the disbelief couldn't keep up with the evidence.

That's how the trust got built. Not trust that nothing hard

will ever happen inside me again. Trust that if it does, it doesn't automatically mean everything is collapsing. Trust that the feeling, however awful, is not the emergency my body keeps insisting it is. Trust that I've been here before and come back every time. It's a quieter kind of trust than the kind I had as a kid, when I trusted reality without even knowing I was doing it. This trust I had to build by hand, plank by plank, out of evidence. But built trust holds weight too. Sometimes it holds better, because you know exactly what it's made of.

And then there are the glimpses. I want to spend real time on these, because they're the part that gives me the most hope, and hope is the thing I most want to hand to whoever is reading this.

Even now, in the in-between, there are moments where it lifts. Not for long. Sometimes only for minutes. But there are moments where the glass thins out and I'm just there. Present. Real. Inside my own life the way I used to be without trying, the way that boy in the first chapter was every single day without ever knowing it was a gift.

They tend to come when I'm doing something I love. That's the pattern I've noticed. Not when I'm trying to feel real—trying never works, trying is just the loop wearing a different coat—but when I'm so absorbed in something I care about that I forget to check whether I feel real, and then look up to discover that I do. It sneaks in the side door, while my attention is somewhere better.

There's one I keep returning to. Senior sunset.

It's a small thing, if you describe it from the outside. A bunch of us, near the end of it all, out together the way you are when something is ending and everyone can feel it. And we started playing pop-up tackle—just a ball, and the simple, stupid, wonderful game of whoever has it runs until they get taken down, and then someone else grabs it and runs, and you chase each other around and crash into the grass and get up laughing and do it again. That's it. That's the whole thing. A ball and my friends and a game with almost no rules, in the last of the daylight.

And for about an hour, I felt real.

I don't mean I distracted myself from the feeling. I mean it was gone. For that hour, there was no glass. No distance. No checking, no scanning, no part of me standing behind the rest of me keeping watch. There was just the ball, and my friends, and my own body running and laughing and getting knocked into the grass, fully there, fully inside the moment, the way I used to be inside every moment before any of this started. I wasn't watching my life from the outside. I was in it. All the way in it.

I want you to see why that hour undid me a little, in the best way. Because that boy—the one playing pop-up tackle in the last light with his friends—that was him. That was the boy from the first chapter. The one who turned roads into racetracks and woods into unexplored territory. The one who, I wrote, wanted in on every game, who threw himself into things completely, who hated losing because he cared, who was so fully present in his life that he never once thought to ask whether he was present at all. I thought that boy was gone. I had spent chapters mourning him like someone who had died. And then, for one hour, with a ball and some friends and no rules, he came back. He was right there. He was me again.

One hour. And I know an hour doesn't sound like much. To someone who has never lived in the glass, an hour of feeling normal is nothing, is invisible, is just an ordinary evening with friends. But to me, that hour was enormous. That hour was proof. That hour was the boy from the first chapter walking around in my body again, reminding me he didn't die. He got buried. There's a difference. And every glimpse since has been another small dig down toward him, another reminder that he's still there under all of it, still real, waiting for the ground to soften enough for him to climb back out.

The glimpses don't last. I want to be honest about that, because I'd be doing you a disservice to pretend that senior sunset fixed me and the credits rolled. The hour ended. We stopped playing. The light went. And somewhere in the next day, the glass came back, the numbness returned, quieter but there, the way it's there most days. That's the in-between. You get the glimpse and you lose it and you get it again. You feel real for an hour and then you don't, and then, some other day, doing some other thing you love, you do again. It is not a straight climb out. It is a series of glimpses, scattered through a lot of quiet management, each one proving a little more than the last that the door isn't locked.

Senior sunset isn't the only one. I want to name another, because it's the one that keeps proving itself, again and again, in a quieter and steadier way than a single evening ever could.

Spending time with my partner makes me feel alive again.

Not in the loud, all-at-once way of a game in the last light. It's gentler than that, and more reliable. There's something about being with the person I love—just being near them, talking, sitting together, existing in the same space—that pulls me back into my own life almost without my noticing. The glass thins. The distance closes. I'll be with them and realize, at some point, that I haven't checked on myself in a while, that

I haven't been scanning, that I've just been here, present, real, inside the moment with them instead of watching it from one step back. Connection does that. It turns out the loop has a hard time running when I'm genuinely reaching toward another person, because reaching outward is the opposite of the inward spiral that feeds it.

I think that's worth saying plainly for anyone reading this who feels as cut off as I did in the worst of it. There was a stretch—I wrote about it earlier—where I genuinely wondered why I should bother connecting with anyone, since I couldn't even be sure they were real. Where the unreality had drained the point out of other people. And here I am now telling you that other people, that one person especially, are one of the most reliable ways I come back to feeling real at all. The very thing the illness tried to convince me was pointless turned out to be part of the cure. Love didn't fix the DPDR. But love is one of the places it loses its grip, every time, and that's not nothing. That's close to everything.

Because that's what the glimpses taught me that nothing else could. They proved the feeling of being real is still available to me. It's not gone. It's not destroyed. The wiring still works—I felt it work, at senior sunset, for an hour; I feel it work, in a quieter way, every time I'm with the person I love. Which means the problem was never that I'd permanently lost the ability to feel real. The problem is that something keeps getting in the way of it, most of the time, and the glimpses are the moments the obstruction clears. And if it can clear for an hour, it can clear for two. If it can clear at senior sunset, or beside my partner, it can clear somewhere else, some other day. The glimpses are the evidence that the door isn't locked. It's just heavy. And I keep finding, here and there, that I can get it open.

I'm also not doing this alone anymore, and that might be the biggest difference of all between this chapter and the early ones.

In the chapters about the worst of it, I was almost entirely alone inside it. A few people knew a little. My mom had seen the worst, once, on the couch. But the day-to-day carrying of it was mine and mine only, done in silence, behind the performance, behind the "yeah, I'm fine, why." That isolation was half of what made it so unbearable. It's one thing to suffer. It's another thing to suffer while convincing everyone around you that nothing is wrong.

Now I have a corner. My mom, still—always. Friends who know now, who I don't have to fully perform for, who I can be the real version around. And a therapist, someone whose whole role is to stand outside the loop with me and help me see it. I am not carrying this by myself anymore, and the weight of a thing changes completely depending on how many hands are under it. The thing itself didn't get that much lighter. I just stopped being the only one holding it. And it turns out that makes nearly all the difference.

I still lose hold of all of this regularly. I want to keep being honest right to the end of the chapter. There are days I slip back into the old thinking and feel like I'm starting over—days the numbness is thick, days I catch myself checking again, days the disbelief comes back and whispers that the doctors were wrong and this really is permanent after all. But I'm learning not to treat those days as resets. They're not a reversal of the process. They're part of it. The in-between isn't a straight climb. It's a place with weather, and some days the weather is bad, and bad weather is not the same as the storm coming back. A hard day is not chapter one again. It just feels like it for a while, until it passes, the way they all have passed.

And even when I can't believe any of this in the moment, I come back to it afterward. That's the part that's actually different now, the part I hold onto hardest.

Because I always come back now, in a way I didn't used to.

There was a time when going into that loop meant staying in it—hours, days, swallowed whole, no exit I could find. Now I go in and I come back out. Sometimes quickly. Sometimes slowly. Sometimes I don't even notice the exact moment it lifts; I just realize later that I'm already on the other side of it again. But I come back. Every time, so far, I have come back. And a person who keeps coming back is not a person who is losing. A person who keeps coming back is a person who is, slowly and unspectacularly, learning how to stay.

People sometimes ask what I want for the future now, like surviving something is supposed to come with a five-year plan and a list of dreams. And I'll be honest about my answer, because honesty is the only thing this book has to offer that a thousand other books don't.

I'm not thinking that far ahead. I'm just getting through each day.

I used to feel like I had to apologize for that. Like an answer that small was a failure of ambition, proof I still wasn't well. I don't feel that way anymore. Getting through each day, when you've lived where I've lived, is not a small ambition. It's the whole ambition. It's the realest, most honest goal I have, and it's one I can actually meet. I'm not trying to map out the next decade of a mind I'm still learning to trust. I'm trying to do today. And then, tomorrow, I'm going to try to do tomorrow. That's the plan. That's the entire plan, and for the first time, the plan is one I can keep.

There's a freedom in that I didn't expect. When the only goal is to get through the day, every day you get through is a win. I'm not measuring myself against the person I was before April 17th anymore, and I'm not measuring myself against some fully recovered version of me that lives in the future. I'm just here, doing this day, and then the next one. And the days keep adding up. That's the quiet arithmetic of the in-between: one managed day, plus one managed day, plus one more, and somehow you look back and there's a whole stretch of them behind you that you survived without noticing you were surviving.

And maybe that's its own kind of hope—not the bright, certain kind I had as a kid, but a smaller, tougher version that holds up better under weight. I don't know exactly what's ahead. I've stopped pretending I need to. What I know is that I've gotten through every single day so far, including the ones I was sure I wouldn't, and that track record is the closest thing to a guarantee I've got. If I got through all of those, I can probably get through the next one. And the next one is all I'm actually being asked to do.

So this isn't the chapter where I tell you I made it out. I haven't made it out. I'm still here, still in it, still learning in real time how to live alongside a mind that doesn't always feel like solid ground. The numbness still visits. The detachment still visits. Most days carry some quiet version of the feeling I've spent this whole book trying to describe, and I manage it, quietly, all day, the way I've learned to.

But it's quieter now. The fires are flickers. The room is bigger. There are glimpses where the boy from the first chapter walks around in me again, playing pop-up tackle in the last light, fully alive. There are people in my corner who believed me. There's a truth I'm slowly coming to trust—that it isn't dangerous, that it isn't permanent—and a growing pile of evidence, written in my own life, that keeps voting for that truth and against the loop.

I'm still not past any of it.

But I'm not where I started.

And that space in between—the quiet, weathered, glimmering, exhausting, hopeful space between the storm and whatever comes next—is where I'm learning how to stay.

For now, staying is enough.

For now, staying is everything.

7

Mind Isn't Mine

There was a point where the scariest part wasn't even the anxiety itself—it was the feeling of not fully recognizing myself inside it. Like I could think my thoughts, but they didn't feel like they belonged to me in the same way anymore. Not because I didn't know who I was, but because my awareness of myself became so intense that it almost started to feel unfamiliar. Like I was watching my own life happen from just slightly outside of it, even while I was still technically living it.

And I remember how hard it was to explain that without it sounding like something bigger than what I was actually experiencing in the moment. Because internally, it wasn't dramatic all the time. It wasn't always loud. Sometimes it was subtle. A shift in perception. A sense of distance. A feeling of being slightly "off" in my own skin. But the fear that followed it made it feel bigger than it was.

That fear was what shaped everything at first.

I used to immediately assume that if I didn't feel fully grounded, then something was wrong with me. Not just temporarily wrong, but fundamentally wrong. Like I was slipping away from myself in a permanent way. That belief made every moment of detachment feel dangerous, even when nothing else around me supported that idea.

But I've had enough experiences now to start separating the feeling from the story I attach to it.

The feeling can still show up. I can still feel slightly distant sometimes, like I'm observing instead of fully immersed. But I don't automatically assume that means I'm losing control anymore. That assumption used to be instant, like a reflex I couldn't interrupt. Now there are times where I can notice the sensation and not immediately escalate it into something larger.

And that pause changes everything.

Because it gives me a moment where I don't have to become the fear.

There are still ups and downs. Still days where I feel more present and days where I feel less present. Still moments where my mind gets loud again and tries to pull me back into old patterns of checking, analyzing, and trying to confirm whether I'm okay or not. And I still slip into that sometimes without realizing it until I'm already in it.

But I also don't stay there the same way anymore.

That's what I keep coming back to.

Not that I never feel it.

Not that I never struggle with it.

But I don't disappear into it as easily as I used to.

And even when I do get pulled in, there's usually a point now where I come back out of it again. Sometimes quickly. Sometimes slowly. Sometimes without even noticing the exact moment it shifts back.

I used to think recovery would feel like never going back into those states again. Like once I understood it, it would just stop happening. But I've learned that it doesn't work like that for me. It's more like learning how to navigate something that can still show up but doesn't have the same power over me when it does.

And that distinction matters more than I used to realize.

Because it means I'm not fragile in the way I thought I was.

It means my mind can feel unstable at times without everything collapsing.

It means I can feel unfamiliar with myself and still return to myself.

And I'm still learning how to trust that.

Still learning how to stay.

There are still moments I have to remind myself that fear is not always information. It feels like it is, especially when it shows up quickly, especially when it attaches itself to a physical sensation or a shift in awareness. My mind still has a way of making everything feel urgent when I'm overwhelmed. Like I need to interpret it immediately or I won't be okay. That urgency is something I've had to slowly learn how to sit beside instead of obey.

And sitting beside it is still not always easy.

Because even now, when something feels slightly off internally, there's still a part of me that wants to tighten everything up right away. To check. To analyze. To make sure I'm not slipping back into something I've already been through. That reflex doesn't fully disappear just because I understand it better. It just becomes something I notice sooner than I used to.

And noticing it sooner changes the outcome.

Not always.

But often enough that I can see the difference.

There are still ups and downs in how I experience myself. Still moments where I feel grounded and moments where I feel slightly detached. Still days where I feel fully present and days where I feel like I'm existing just a bit behind my own eyes instead of fully inside them. And I don't always know why those shifts happen. Sometimes they correlate with stress. Sometimes they don't seem to correlate with anything at all.

That used to scare me more than anything.

Because I needed patterns. I needed explanations. I needed certainty that I could predict what was happening inside me. But my mind doesn't always work in predictable patterns, especially under pressure. And trying to force it into one only made me more hyper-aware of every change, which made everything feel louder.

So I've had to unlearn that need, slowly.

Not completely.

But enough to function differently inside it.

Now, when something shifts internally, I don't always immediately turn it into a full investigation. Sometimes I just notice it. Sometimes I acknowledge it without building a narrative around it. Sometimes I keep doing what I was already doing instead of stopping everything to figure myself out.

And those small decisions are what changed things over time.

Because they taught me that I don't always have to respond to everything inside me as if it's an emergency.

Even when it feels like one.

Even when my mind insists it is.

There are still moments where I slip back into old habits. Where I start checking myself again without meaning to. Where I start analyzing every thought and sensation like I need to confirm I'm okay. And in those moments, I still have to catch myself and step back out of it.

But I can step back out now.

That's the difference.

I don't stay trapped in the loop the way I used to. I don't lose entire stretches of time to it the same way. I don't always spiral from a single feeling into a full collapse of meaning. It can still happen in pieces, but it doesn't take everything with it anymore.

And I've started to recognize that as progress, even when it doesn't feel like the kind of progress I expected.

Because I thought healing would feel like never going back there at all.

But for me, it looks more like returning less deeply.

Returning less often.

And coming back out faster than before.

And I'm still learning how to trust that.

Still learning how to stay.

There's something strange about getting used to your own mind not always feeling like home. Not in a constant way, not in a dramatic way, but in a quiet awareness that sometimes things inside you will feel slightly unfamiliar, and you'll have to keep living anyway. I don't think I understood at first that this was what it would become—not a fixed state, but a learning process that I would keep revisiting in different forms.

And I've had to stop treating that unfamiliarity like it automatically means danger.

That was one of the hardest habits to break.

Because my brain learned early on to treat internal shifts like warnings. If I felt different, I assumed something was wrong. If I felt detached, I assumed I was losing control. If I felt too aware of myself, I assumed it meant I was slipping into something I couldn't come back from. And that pattern made every small change feel like a threat, even when nothing external was actually happening.

But I've had enough repetition now to see that not every shift leads somewhere worse.

Sometimes it just passes.

Sometimes it's just fatigue or stress or my nervous system reacting in a way I don't fully understand in the moment. And I don't always need to solve it to get through it. That idea still doesn't feel natural all the time, but it's becoming more familiar than it used to be.

There are still ups and downs. Still moments where I feel more grounded and moments where I feel slightly disconnected. Still times where I catch myself over-analyzing everything internally without meaning to. And even though I recognize those patterns more quickly now, that doesn't mean I never fall into them anymore.

I still do.

Just not in the same way.

Not as deeply.

Not as all-consuming.

And not for as long.

That's the part I keep noticing in hindsight more than in real time. Because in the moment, it can still feel like I'm in it again. Like I'm back in that space where everything feels uncertain and I start questioning what I'm feeling and why

I'm feeling it. But afterward, I can see that I came out of it sooner than I would have before. That I didn't escalate it as far. That I didn't lose the entire day to it the way I used to.

And that matters, even if it doesn't feel dramatic.

Because my definition of "okay" has had to change.

It used to mean never feeling this way at all.

Now it means being able to feel it and still continue.

Still function.

Still come back.

Still not let it define everything.

And I think that shift has been the most important part of all of this.

Not eliminating the experience.

But changing what it gets to take from me.

I'm still not where I want to be all the time. I still have moments that are hard, moments that feel uncertain, moments where I have to remind myself that I've been through this before and come out of it again. But I also don't lose myself in those moments the way I used to.

And that's something I can't ignore anymore.

Even if it's not perfect.

Even if it's still in progress.

I'm still here.

And I'm still learning how to stay.

I've started to realize that a lot of what I experience now isn't about trying to get rid of certain feelings but learning how not to build entire conclusions around them in real time. That's been one of the biggest internal shifts for me, even though it doesn't always feel obvious while it's happening. My mind still produces moments where I feel slightly off, slightly distant, or overly aware of myself in a way that used to immediately trigger fear. But now, those moments don't automatically turn into a full internal collapse the way they used to.

That didn't happen because the feelings stopped showing up. It happened because my reaction to them slowly changed.

There are still times where I catch myself starting to spiral internally without even noticing the exact moment it begins. It can start very small, like a single sensation or thought that feels unfamiliar, and then my mind begins doing what it was trained to do for a long time—scan, analyze, try to confirm whether I'm okay or not. That process used to feel automatic and uncontrollable, like once it started, there was no stopping it until it ran its course.

Now, I sometimes notice it earlier.

Not always.

But often enough that I can interrupt it.

And even when I don't interrupt it in time, it doesn't always build the same way anymore. It doesn't always escalate into the same intensity. Sometimes it stays contained. Sometimes it fades. Sometimes I realize later that I was briefly back in that mindset but didn't fully lose myself inside it.

That realization has been important for me, because it challenges the way I used to define setbacks. Before, if I had any moment like that, I would see it as proof that nothing had changed. As if progress only counted if it was permanent and uninterrupted. But I don't see it that way anymore, because my actual lived experience doesn't match that idea.

I still have ups and downs. I still have days where I feel more grounded and days where I feel less grounded. I still have moments where I feel slightly detached from myself, like I'm observing my life instead of fully feeling inside it. And

I don't want to pretend those moments are gone, because they're not. They're still part of how my mind responds under stress or overload.

But they don't define everything anymore.

That's the part I keep returning to.

Because even when those feelings show up, they don't automatically take over the entire structure of my day. They don't always become the only thing I can think about. They don't always turn into hours of spiraling or constant checking. Sometimes they pass in the background while I continue doing what I need to do, even if I don't feel perfectly aligned inside myself.

And I've had to learn that that still counts as progress.

Not because it looks perfect from the outside, but because it represents a different kind of relationship with my own mind. One where I'm not constantly trying to force certainty out of every feeling. One where I can experience something uncomfortable and not immediately turn it into a conclusion about myself or my future.

That shift didn't happen quickly, and it still isn't fully stable. But it's real enough now that I can see it when I look back.

And I think that's what matters most.

Not that I never struggle.

But I don't always lose myself in it anymore.

There are still moments where I have to deal with the fact that my mind doesn't always feel predictable, and I've stopped expecting it to be. That expectation used to be something I held onto tightly, even when I didn't realize it. I thought that if I could just understand myself enough, if I could just learn the pattern well enough, then I would be able to prevent the uncomfortable moments from happening in the first place.

But that's not how my mind works, and it never really was.

What's changed is that I don't treat unpredictability as automatically dangerous anymore.

There are still internal shifts that catch my attention. A moment where I feel slightly disconnected, or where my awareness of myself becomes sharper than usual, or where my thoughts feel a little less anchored than I would like. For example, I recall many times where I would attempt to prove my existence, that I'm real. It never worked; therefore, I would uncontrollably panic, creating SI that would creep in. Those moments still exist. But they don't always trigger the same immediate reaction they used to. They don't always turn into fear right away. Sometimes they just stay as they are for a bit before fading again on their own. Sometimes I do panic. I am not—although hard—working on being perfect but on progression, and sometimes is progression when it was never.

I've had to learn that not everything needs to be controlled to be survivable.

That's still something I'm working through. Because even now, when something feels unfamiliar internally, there's still a part of me that wants to grab onto it and figure it out immediately. To analyze it. To label it. To decide what it means before it has a chance to become anything else. That reflex is still there, especially when I'm stressed or overwhelmed or not fully grounded.

But I don't always follow it anymore.

Sometimes I notice it forming and choose not to engage with it fully. Not because I'm ignoring myself, but because I've learned what that engagement usually leads to for me. It leads to more scanning, more questioning, more tightening of my attention inward until everything feels louder than it actually is. And I've lived through that enough times now to recognize that it doesn't actually help me feel safer in the long run.

So I've started practicing something different, even if I don't always have a name for it in the moment. It's more like allowing space between what I feel and what I decide about it. A small pause where I don't immediately turn sensation into meaning. And in that pause, things often don't escalate the way they used to.

There are still ups and downs. Still days where I feel more grounded and days where I feel less grounded. Still moments where I feel slightly outside myself, like I'm observing instead of fully being inside my own experience. And even though I recognize those moments more clearly now, they can still feel uncomfortable while they're happening.

But they don't always expand anymore.

That's what I keep noticing.

They don't always turn into the same cycle. They don't always take over everything. Sometimes they just pass through, and I continue on with my day even if I don't feel perfectly steady inside it. And afterward, I can see that I didn't lose myself the way I used to.

That's not something I would have believed at the beginning of this.

Because at the beginning, every shift felt final. Every uncomfortable moment felt like proof that I was slipping backward. Every sense of detachment felt like I was losing something permanent. But I've lived through enough of those moments now to know that they aren't final, even when they feel that way.

And I think that's the part I'm still learning to trust.

Not that the feelings won't come.

But that they don't get to decide everything when they do.

I've had to accept that my mind is always going to have moments that feel unfamiliar, and that acceptance didn't come from everything getting easier—it came from realizing I couldn't keep living in constant reaction to every internal shift. There were too many moments where I tried to solve my way out of myself, and all it really did was make me more afraid of my own thoughts and sensations. At some point, I started to see that the cycle wasn't just the feelings themselves but the way I responded to them.

That response is what has slowly changed.

There are still moments where I feel slightly disconnected, like I'm not fully anchored in myself in the way I want to be. There are still moments where my awareness becomes sharper than I'm comfortable with, where I start noticing myself instead of just existing naturally inside my own experience. And even now, that can feel unsettling for a second. It can still pull my attention inward in a way that feels familiar, even if it doesn't escalate the same way it used to.

But it doesn't always turn into fear anymore.

That's the part I keep coming back to.

Because there was a time when that feeling meant everything. If I felt off, then I *was* off. If I felt distant, then something was wrong. If I felt disconnected, then I assumed I was losing control completely. There was no separation between experience and interpretation. They were the same thing in my mind, and that made everything heavier than it needed to be.

Now, there's a separation forming.

Not perfectly.

Not consistently.

But enough that I can notice it.

Sometimes I feel something and don't immediately assign it meaning. Sometimes I experience a shift internally and don't turn it into a prediction about what's going to happen next. Sometimes I can let a moment exist without trying to force it into certainty right away. And in those moments, I don't spiral the way I used to.

That doesn't mean I'm never affected by it. I still have ups and downs. I still have days where I feel more grounded and days where I feel less grounded. I still have moments where I slip into old patterns without realizing it at first. But even those moments don't define everything anymore.

They pass.

And I come back.

Sometimes quickly, sometimes slowly, but I come back.

And I've started to understand that that matters more than whether the feeling shows up in the first place. Because I can't fully control every internal experience I have, but I am learning that I don't have to disappear into them anymore either.

I don't have to run every time my mind feels unfamiliar.

I don't have to turn every sensation into a conclusion.

I don't have to treat every shift as if it means something permanent about me.

I can just let it pass.

And still stay.

Even when it doesn't feel perfect.

Even when it doesn't feel certain.

Even when my mind still doesn't feel fully like mine.

I'm still here.

And I'm still learning how to stay.

8

Aftermath

I don't think there was ever a single moment where everything just went back to normal for me, because what I went through didn't really leave a clean "before and after" line in my life. It changed how I experience everything in smaller ways that don't always look obvious from the outside. Most people would probably see me functioning and assume things are just fine, and in a lot of ways they are, but internally there's still a level of awareness I carry that didn't exist before all of this started.

And I've had to learn not to resent that.

Because at first I did.

At first I thought I was supposed to go back to who I was before, like the goal was to erase everything I had experienced internally and return to some version of normal that existed earlier in my life. But over time I started realizing that wasn't realistic for me. I can't un-know what my mind has done. I can't un-feel what I've felt. And I can't fully erase the way I now notice myself thinking and reacting.

So instead of trying to go back, I've been learning how to

move forward with it still existing in the background.

There are still moments where I feel slightly detached from myself, like I'm observing my life instead of fully being inside it. And even though those moments don't always escalate anymore, I still notice them when they show up. They still catch my attention for a second. But I don't always interpret them as danger now. That part has changed slowly over time, even if I didn't notice it happening in real time.

Now, sometimes I just let it be there.

I don't always try to fix it immediately.

I don't always try to analyze it until it makes sense.

Sometimes I just continue what I'm doing and let the moment pass on its own.

And I've had to learn that nothing falls apart when I do that.

That was one of the hardest things to accept, because so much of my earlier experience was built on the belief that I had to constantly monitor myself in order to stay okay. That if I stopped paying attention for even a moment, something might spiral out of control. But I've lived through enough of those moments now to know that isn't true in the way I thought it was.

There are still ups and downs. Still days where I feel more grounded and days where I feel less grounded. Still moments where my mind gets louder again and I start to feel that familiar pull inward. But those moments don't automatically become everything anymore. They don't define the full structure of my day like they used to.

And that's the difference I keep noticing.

Not that the feelings disappeared.

But that they don't get to take over the same way.

And I think that matters more than I used to understand.

Because I used to think healing would mean never feeling like this again. Never feeling detached. Never feeling anxious. Never feeling uncertain inside my own mind. But now I understand that for me, it's more about what happens after those feelings show up.

Whether I stay inside them.

Or whether I come back out.

And I do come back out now.

Even when it takes time.

Even when it's not perfect.

Even when it still doesn't feel fully easy.

I still come back.

And I'm still here.

There are parts of this experience that I still don't have perfect language for, not because I don't understand them anymore, but because they don't fit neatly into explanations that make sense when you try to say them out loud. It's more like living with shifts in perception that don't always announce themselves clearly. Sometimes it's subtle, like I'm slightly less "inside" myself than usual. Other times it's more noticeable, like I'm aware of my own thoughts in a way that feels too sharp or too distant at the same time.

And I've learned that not every one of those moments needs to become a problem to solve.

That's still something I have to actively remind myself of.

Because my mind still tries to interpret everything. It still wants meaning immediately. It still wants certainty. And when I'm tired or stressed, that old system becomes louder again, like it's trying to pull me back into the same cycle I used to live in full time. The scanning starts. The checking starts. The internal questioning starts. And for a moment, it can feel like I'm right back in it again.

But I'm not.

Not in the same way.

Because now there's something else that exists alongside it. A level of awareness that I didn't have before. A part of me that can recognize, even while it's happening, that this is a familiar pattern. That I've been here before. That I don't have to follow it all the way down just because it showed up.

And sometimes that recognition is enough to change the direction of it.

Not always immediately.

Not perfectly.

But enough that things don't escalate the way they used to.

There are still ups and downs in how I experience all of this. Still days where I feel more grounded and days where I feel less grounded. Still moments where I feel slightly disconnected from myself, like I'm watching instead of fully participating. And even though I can recognize those states more quickly now, they can still feel uncomfortable in the moment. That part hasn't fully gone away.

What's changed is what I believe those moments mean.

Before, they meant everything was falling apart.

Now, they don't automatically mean anything at all.

Sometimes they're just states.

Sometimes they're just passing experiences.

Sometimes they don't require any explanation beyond the fact that they happened.

And I've had to slowly learn how to let that be true without trying to override it with fear.

That's not easy for me. It never became easy overnight.

I don't think I fully understood at the beginning that

recovery would still include the memory of what it felt like to not feel okay. I thought it would fade in a way where I wouldn't think about it anymore, where it would just become something distant and unrelated to how I live now. But that's not really how it works for me. It's more like it stays in the background as something I can recognize, but it doesn't control the foreground anymore.

And that difference is subtle, but it's everything.

There are still moments where I feel slightly outside myself, like I'm aware of my own thoughts in a way that makes them feel more distant than usual. Not always in a distressing way anymore, but still noticeable. And even when it does feel uncomfortable, it doesn't automatically turn into the same chain reaction it used to. It doesn't always become fear, then panic, then spiraling, then losing hours inside my own head. Sometimes it just stays as a moment that passes through without expanding.

That used to feel impossible.

Because there was a time when I genuinely believed that if I felt that way, it meant I was slipping back into something I wouldn't be able to get out of. But I've had enough experiences now to know that's not how it actually plays out. I've felt those same sensations and still continued my day. I've felt disconnected and still come back to myself later. I've had moments that felt intense in real time and then looked completely different in hindsight.

And that has slowly changed what I trust.

Not in the sense that I never get shaken anymore.

But in the sense that I don't immediately assume I'm losing everything when I do.

There are still ups and downs. Still days where I feel more

grounded and days where I feel less grounded. Still moments where my mind gets louder and I have to work harder to stay present inside my own life instead of getting pulled inward. And I don't want to write this in a way that erases those parts, because they're still real. They're still part of my experience.

But they don't define me the same way anymore.

That's what I keep noticing.

The feeling can show up, but it doesn't always decide what everything means now.

And that's a shift I didn't think I would reach when I was in the middle of it.

Because in the beginning, everything felt absolute. Either I was okay or I wasn't. Either I was grounded or I wasn't. Either I was in control or I wasn't. There wasn't much room for anything in between those extremes. But now I live more in the in-between than anything else. Not fully stable, not fully unstable—just learning how to move through both without losing myself in either one.

And I think that's the part that matters most.

Not that everything stopped happening.

But it stopped owning me when it did.

I'm still here.

Still learning.

Still staying.

9

Inside My Mind

I think at some point I stopped waiting for everything inside me to feel perfectly aligned before I could live my life again. There was a time where I believed I needed internal stability first—complete clarity, complete grounding, complete certainty—before I could fully show up as myself. But the longer I lived through everything I've described, the more I realized that kind of condition never actually arrives in the way you expect it to.

So I had to start learning how to live without it.

That didn't mean giving up on feeling better. It meant changing what "better" even looked like for me. Because if better meant never feeling detached again, never feeling anxious again, never feeling uncertain again, then I was setting myself up for something I couldn't realistically maintain. But if better meant being able to feel those things and still continue, still function, still stay connected to my life in some way—that was something I could actually move toward.

And slowly, I have.

There are still moments where I feel slightly outside myself.

Not in a way that defines everything anymore, but in a way that I notice and recognize quickly. A shift in awareness, a subtle distance, a moment where I become more conscious of my own thinking than I am of just existing inside it. Those moments still happen, and I don't want to pretend they don't.

But I don't always treat them like they're breaking news anymore.

That's what's changed the most.

I don't immediately assume I need to fix everything about myself just because something feels different internally. I don't always turn every sensation into a full analysis of my mental state. Sometimes I just let it exist without adding more weight to it than it already has. And sometimes, it passes without ever becoming anything bigger than a passing moment.

That used to feel impossible to me.

Because for so long, I was operating under the belief that control was the same thing as safety. That if I could just monitor myself closely enough, I could prevent anything bad from happening internally. But what I've learned instead is that constant monitoring didn't actually give me more control—it just made me more afraid of everything I was noticing.

So I've had to slowly step back from that pattern.

Not all at once.

Not perfectly.

But enough to change how I move through my own thoughts.

There are still ups and downs. Still days where I feel more grounded and days where I feel less grounded. Still moments where my mind gets loud again, and I have to remind myself not to follow every thought as if it were absolute truth in that moment. And I still slip sometimes. I still fall back into old ways of thinking when I'm overwhelmed or tired or not fully present.

But I don't stay there the same way anymore.

That's the difference I keep coming back to.

It doesn't take me over as completely. It doesn't define everything I am in that moment. It doesn't erase everything I've learned before it. It's just something I move through now, instead of something I disappear into.

And I think that's what this has really become for me.

Not a story about everything going away.

But a story about learning how to stay inside my own life even when my mind doesn't always feel steady.

I'm still here.

Still learning.

Still living inside it.

There are still days where I can feel the weight of everything I've been through without it needing to be loud or overwhelming. It's not always panic anymore. It's not always fear. Sometimes it's just a quiet awareness that my mind has changed in ways I can't fully undo and that I've had to adapt to that in real time while still trying to live a normal life on the outside.

And that kind of awareness can be strange to carry.

Because most people don't see it.

Most people only see what's visible—how I talk, how I show up, how I function in everyday life. They don't see the internal moments where I pause for a second longer than usual because something inside me feels slightly unfamiliar. They don't see the moments where I have to gently redirect my thoughts back to the present instead of letting them spiral inward. They don't see the effort it sometimes takes just to stay steady in something that looks completely ordinary from the outside.

But I feel it.

And I've had to learn how to not let that awareness turn into something that isolates me from my own life.

There are still ups and downs. Still moments where I feel more grounded and moments where I feel slightly disconnected. Still times where I notice myself slipping into old patterns of overthinking or internal checking, especially when I'm stressed or overwhelmed. And even though I recognize those patterns more quickly now, I don't always avoid them entirely.

Sometimes I still fall into them.

But I don't stay in them as long.

That's something I've had to learn to notice carefully, because progress like that doesn't always feel dramatic while it's happening. It often feels like nothing is changing at all until you look back and realize the cycles aren't as long, the intensity isn't as strong, and the recovery is a little faster than it used to be. It's not one big moment of transformation—it's repetition. It's accumulation. It's slowly building a different response over time.

And I think that's what's happened for me.

Not the removal of struggle.

But a change in how long it holds me.

There are still moments where I feel slightly outside myself, like I'm observing instead of fully being inside my experience. And even though I've learned not to immediately panic when that happens, I still notice it. I still feel it. It still briefly shifts how I relate to the moment I'm in. But it doesn't always become something bigger anymore.

Sometimes it just passes.

Sometimes I continue my day while it's there.

Sometimes I don't even fully register when it leaves.

And that used to feel impossible to imagine.

Because there was a time when I thought every shift like that meant I was losing control again. I thought it meant I was going backward. I thought it meant everything I had gone through would just repeat itself in the same way, over and over. But I've learned that repetition doesn't mean exact return. It doesn't mean I'm starting over every time something familiar shows up.

It just means I still have a mind that reacts.

And I'm still learning how to respond differently to it.

Not perfectly.

Not all the time.

But more than before.

And that's what I keep holding onto.

Not that I never struggle anymore.

But I don't disappear inside it the way I used to.

I stay longer now.

I come back faster.

And I'm still here.

I don't think I can separate my growth from the parts of this that still feel uncomfortable. They're not two different stories for me. They exist together in the same space, sometimes on the same day, sometimes even within the same hour. I can feel okay, then slightly off, then okay again without there necessarily being a clear reason for any of it. And I've had to stop expecting consistency from my internal world in order to make peace with the fact that it doesn't always offer it.

That was a difficult adjustment.

Because at first I interpreted inconsistency as instability in the worst sense. I thought if I wasn't feeling steady all the time, then I wasn't actually improving. But over time I started realizing that stability, at least for me, doesn't mean never shifting. It means being able to shift without everything collapsing around it.

There are still ups and downs. Still moments where I feel more grounded and moments where I feel less grounded. There are still times when my mind gets louder and I have to work a little harder to stay present instead of getting pulled inward. And I don't always succeed at that immediately. Sometimes I still get caught in old patterns without noticing right away. Sometimes I still overanalyze what I'm feeling and start building meaning around things that don't need meaning in that moment.

But even then, something is different now.

Because I don't lose myself as easily inside it.

That's the part I keep noticing when I look back. The same kinds of sensations can still show up, the same kinds of thoughts can still pass through, but they don't always expand the way they used to. They don't always take over everything in the same way. Sometimes they stay small. Sometimes they pass. Sometimes I realize afterward that I moved through them without fully spiraling into them at all.

And I've had to learn not to dismiss that just because it doesn't feel dramatic.

There was a time where I thought progress had to feel obvious in order to be real. Like I needed a clear before-and-after version of myself to prove that anything had changed. But what I've learned instead is that change like this is often quiet. It shows up in how quickly I recover, in how often I catch myself before I spiral, in how many moments I can stay present even when I don't feel perfectly aligned inside.

Those things don't always feel like progress in real time.

But they are.

There are still moments where I feel slightly detached from myself, like I'm observing instead of fully immersed in what I'm doing. And even though I recognize that feeling more quickly now, it can still be uncomfortable while it's happening. It can still pull my attention inward for a second. It can still make me question what I'm feeling.

But it doesn't always turn into something bigger anymore.

That's what's changed the most.

Not the absence of those moments.

But the absence of what they used to become.

And I think that's what I've been learning all along, even when I didn't have the words for it yet.

Not how to stop feeling this way completely.

But how do I stay present while I do?

And I'm still here.

Still learning.

Still staying.

There's something I've come to understand more clearly the longer I sit with everything I've been through, and it's that pain doesn't always look the way people expect it to look. It doesn't always show up in obvious ways. It doesn't always announce itself. Sometimes it sits quietly underneath everything else, shaping how a person moves through the world without anyone around them fully realizing what's happening internally.

And because of that, I've also learned how unfair it is when people reduce someone's struggle down to weakness.

Because what I've lived through—and what so many people go through in different ways—isn't weakness. It's human overwhelm. It's nervous systems that reach their limit. It's minds trying to survive internal states that feel too heavy to carry alone. And I've seen enough of it, both personally and in others, to know that the people who are struggling are not the ones lacking strength.

If anything, they're the ones enduring more than most people can see.

What hurts more than the struggle itself, sometimes, is the way it gets judged from the outside. The way people who haven't lived inside that kind of internal experience can be quick to label it, minimize it, or turn it into something shameful. And I don't think that's just misunderstanding—it actually makes things heavier for the people already carrying too much.

Because shame doesn't help someone heal.

Understanding does.

Compassion does.

Space to exist without being reduced does.

And I've had to learn, through everything I've experienced, that the people who are hurting are not the problem. The struggle itself is not a moral failure. It's not something that makes someone less than it. It's not something that defines their worth or their strength.

What does say something about us, as people, is how we respond to that pain in others.

Whether we judge it or whether we try to understand it.

Whether we shame it or whether we recognize it as something deeply human.

I've had moments in my own life where I've felt overwhelmed in ways I didn't fully understand at the time, where everything inside me felt too loud and too heavy and too unfamiliar. And in those moments, what made the difference wasn't criticism or fear or judgment—it was support, even when it was small. Even when it was just someone being present. Even when it was just time passing without me being alone in it.

That's what I hold onto now.

Not the idea that people who struggle are broken.

But the idea that they are human.

And that includes me.

Even now, even after everything, I still have ups and downs. Still have moments where I feel more grounded and moments where I feel less grounded. I still have times where my mind feels louder than I want it to be, and I have to work to stay present inside my own life instead of getting pulled inward. But I don't look at those moments as proof that I'm failing anymore.

I look at them as something I move for.

Something I survive.

Something that passes.

And I'm still here.

Still learning.

Still staying.

I don't think I'll ever be able to describe this part of my life as something I've fully "left behind," because even the way I think about myself has been shaped by it. It didn't just pass through like a phase that ended cleanly. It stayed long enough to change how I notice everything—my thoughts, my body, my reactions, and even the quiet moments when nothing is happening but I'm still aware of myself in a different way than I used to be.

And I've had to make peace with the fact that I'm not trying to erase that anymore.

There are still days where I feel slightly disconnected, where my mind feels louder than I want it to, where I catch myself slipping into old patterns of overthinking or internal checking without meaning to. And even though I recognize those patterns more quickly now, they still show up. They're still part of how my brain responds under stress, under fatigue, under pressure. That hasn't disappeared.

But it doesn't define my entire experience anymore.

That's what I keep coming back to.

There are moments now where I can feel something shift internally and not immediately attach fear to it. Moments where I can feel slightly outside myself and not assume it means I'm losing control. Moments where I can notice the familiar patterns starting and not fully follow them down the same path I used to. And even when I do slip back into those patterns, I don't stay there as deeply or as long as I once did.

That change is quiet, but it's real.

And I've had to learn not to dismiss it just because it doesn't feel dramatic.

Because for a long time, I thought healing had to look like a complete absence of struggle. Like I would eventually reach a point where none of this would ever happen again and I would just be "done" with it. But what I understand now is that my experience doesn't work in absolutes like that. It moves. It shifts. It returns in smaller ways sometimes. But it doesn't own me the way it used to.

And that distinction matters more than anything else.

I still have ups and downs. Still have moments where I feel more grounded and moments where I feel less grounded. Still have days where my mind feels calm and days where it feels louder. But those fluctuations don't erase everything else anymore. They don't define who I am or what I'm capable of or how far I've come.

They're just part of the experience.

Not the whole thing.

And I think that's what I've been learning this entire time without fully realizing it in the beginning—not how to eliminate every uncomfortable moment, but how to stop letting those moments decide everything about me.

I'm still learning how to live inside my own mind without fearing every shift.

Still learning how to stay present even when it feels unfamiliar.

Still learning how to come back to myself without panic.

And even now, even with everything I've written and lived through and felt, I'm still here.

Still becoming.

Still staying.

There's a point where I stopped waiting for my internal world to become perfectly quiet before I let myself fully participate in my life again. For a long time, I thought I needed resolution first—like I needed to reach some final state of stability before I could just exist without constantly analyzing myself in the background. But life didn't pause for that. It kept moving, even when I didn't feel fully steady inside it.

And I had to learn how to move with it anyway.

There are still moments where I feel slightly disconnected from myself, where my awareness of my own thoughts becomes sharper than usual, where I catch myself slipping into old habits of checking and scanning without meaning to. Those moments still happen. They aren't gone. They're just no longer the center of everything the way they used to be.

That's what's changed.

Not the presence of struggle, but its position in my life.

I don't automatically build my entire identity around how I feel in a single moment anymore. I don't immediately assume that discomfort means collapse. I don't treat every shift in perception as something that needs to be solved right away in order for me to be okay. Sometimes I just notice it, acknowledge it internally, and keep going with whatever I was already doing.

And that used to feel impossible.

Because there was a time when everything inside me felt like it demanded attention all at once. Every sensation felt important. Every thought felt like it needed interpretation. Every moment of uncertainty felt like something I had to fix immediately or I wouldn't be able to handle what came next. That kind of internal pressure made even normal days feel heavy.

Now, it doesn't always do that.

There are still ups and downs. Still days where I feel more grounded and days where I feel less grounded. Still moments where I feel slightly outside myself, like I'm observing instead of fully inside the experience. But even those moments don't always spiral the same way anymore. They don't always expand into something bigger. Sometimes they just pass through and leave without taking everything with them.

And I've started to recognize that as something real, even when it feels subtle.

Because I used to think progress had to be obvious to count. I thought I would feel completely different in a way that I could clearly point to and say, "This is when everything changed." But instead, it's been quieter than that. It's noticed that I recover faster. That I don't lose as much time inside my own head. That I can feel something uncomfortable and still stay present in my life at the same time.

Those changes don't always feel dramatic.

But they add up.

And I think that's what I've been learning more than anything else.

Not how to become someone who never struggles.

But how to become someone who doesn't disappear when they do.

And I'm still here.

Still learning.

Still staying.

I think one of the hardest things to explain about all of this is that even when things get better, your mind doesn't just forget what it learned in survival mode. It still remembers how to scan for danger. It still remembers how to tighten around certain sensations. It still remembers how to turn small internal shifts into something that feels bigger than they are. And even when you've grown past the peak of it, those pathways don't just disappear overnight.

They just stop being the only path.

There are still moments where I catch myself slipping into that older way of thinking without realizing it right away. Where I start checking my internal state too closely, where I start questioning what I feel instead of just letting it exist, where I start trying to get certainty out of something that doesn't actually offer certainty in the first place. And for a second, it can feel like I'm back there again.

But I'm not.

Not in the same way.

Because now there's something else that exists alongside it. A kind of awareness that didn't used to be there before. A space where I can notice what's happening without immediately becoming it. A moment where I can recognize the pattern instead of being fully pulled into it. And even if I don't always use that space perfectly, even if I don't always catch it in time, it's there more often than it used to be.

That alone has changed everything.

There are still ups and downs. Still days where I feel more grounded and days where I feel less grounded. Still moments where my mind feels louder, more uncertain, more focused inward than I want it to be. And I don't want to pretend those moments are gone, because they aren't. They still show up in different forms, at different intensities, at different times.

But they don't define everything anymore.

That's the part I keep realizing in hindsight more than in real time.

In the moment, it can still feel uncomfortable. It can still feel like something is shifting in a way I don't fully understand yet. But afterward, I can see that I didn't spiral the way I used to. I can see that I didn't lose myself inside it. I can see that it passed without becoming permanent.

And that's not nothing.

Even if it doesn't always feel like enough in the moment, it matters.

Because it means I'm not living the same experience I was before. It means I'm not trapped in the same reactions. It means I've built some distance between what I feel and what I assume it means about me.

And that distance is what allows me to stay.

Not perfectly.

Not without struggle.

But still here.

Still moving.

Still becoming something that isn't defined by the worst moments anymore.

I don't think there's a version of this where everything feels completely resolved, and I've stopped expecting one. What I've learned instead is that my life doesn't require everything inside me to be perfectly calm in order for me to live it. That was the belief that used to run everything for me in the background—that I needed internal certainty first, and then I could move forward. But that version of life never really arrived. So I had to learn how to live without waiting for it.

And that's what I'm still doing.

There are still moments where my mind feels slightly off from what I want it to feel like. Moments where I notice myself too much. Moments where I feel a little detached, or a little too aware, or a little uncertain in a way that used to send everything into a panic. Those moments still exist. They're still part of my experience. But they don't automatically take over everything anymore.

That's what's changed.

Not the presence of struggle, but the power it holds over me.

There are still ups and downs. Still days where I feel grounded and days where I feel less grounded. Still times where I have to work a little harder to stay present instead of getting pulled inward. And I don't always get it right in the moment. Sometimes I still slip into old patterns without noticing until I'm already in them.

But I come back faster now.

I don't stay lost in it the same way.

And I don't build my entire identity around it anymore.

That used to be the hardest part—how quickly a single internal moment could turn into a full story about who I was, what was wrong with me, what would happen next. Everything felt absolute. Everything felt like it meant something permanent. But I've started learning that most moments aren't permanent. They pass. They shift. They move through me without defining me unless I let them.

And I don't always let them anymore.

Not perfectly.

Not all the time.

But enough.

Enough to notice the difference.

Enough to keep going.

Enough to stay in my life even when my mind doesn't feel completely steady.

And I think that's what this has been about more than anything else.

Not becoming someone who never struggles.

But becoming someone who doesn't disappear when they do.

I'm still here.

Still learning.

Still living inside it.

10

Mad Mind

Before I say anything else, I want to be honest: this chapter is fucking uncomfortable. Not because it contains the darkest moments of my journey, but because it contains emotions people do not always like to admit exist. For a long time, I thought surviving would solve everything. I thought answers would bring peace, progress would erase frustration, and making it through the hardest days would somehow make the anger disappear. It didn't. In many ways, the anger grew. Some of it was directed at other people. Some of it was directed at anxiety. Some of it was directed at the circumstances I found myself living through. And some of it was directed at the person staring back at me in the mirror. The truth is that mental health struggles do not always leave you feeling inspired, grateful, or hopeful. Sometimes they leave you feeling exhausted. Sometimes they leave you feeling frustrated. Sometimes they leave you carrying questions that nobody seems able to answer. This chapter is about that anger—not the kind that explodes, but the kind that lingers. The kind that quietly follows you from room to room, grows in the spaces between appointments and answers, and settles into places you never expected it to. For a long time, I didn't know where to put that anger, so I carried it. These are the places it lived:

***Part I:* They don't understand because you are you, they aren't.**

I wasn't angry because people tried to understand me. I wasn't angry because they cared enough to respond. I was angry because so many people seemed to stop listening the moment they thought they understood. Throughout my mental health journey, I heard the same phrase more times than I can count: "I know exactly what you're going through." Sometimes it came from friends. Sometimes it came from acquaintances. Sometimes it came from people who genuinely wanted to help. The intention was usually good, but the impact was not. Every time I heard those words, it felt as if my story was being interrupted before it was even finished. Instead of hearing me out, people would immediately compare my experience to theirs. The conversation would shift from what I was feeling to what they had once felt. Maybe they were trying to relate. Maybe they thought it would make me feel less alone. But instead, it made me feel unheard.

The frustrating part was that I never claimed to be the only person struggling. I never believed my pain was unique. I understood that everyone faces challenges and that mental health struggles affect millions of people. What angered me was the assumption that my experience could be summarized so quickly. It felt as though people heard a few words and immediately concluded they knew the entire story. They didn't hear about the sleepless nights. They didn't hear about the constant fear. They didn't hear about the doctor's appointments, the uncertainty, the exhaustion, or the endless questions racing through my mind. They heard enough to recognize a piece of their own experience, and suddenly my story became theirs.

Every time someone told me they knew exactly what I was going through, I felt my voice shrink a little more. It wasn't because I wanted sympathy. It wasn't because I wanted special treatment. It was because I wanted to be heard. There is a difference between understanding someone's struggle and assuming you already know everything about it. I wasn't looking for someone to finish my sentences. I was looking for someone willing to sit through them. I wanted someone to listen without comparing, fixing, explaining, or translating my experience into something easier to understand. I wanted someone to simply acknowledge that what I was feeling was real.

There were moments when I felt like I could have told someone that my entire world was falling apart and somehow they would still respond with a story about their own stressful week. That's what made me angry. It felt as though no matter how loudly I spoke, my words never carried enough weight. No matter how carefully I explained what I was experiencing, the response was often the same. Someone would reassure me that they understood, and somehow I would leave the conversation feeling more alone than before. Not because they were trying to hurt me, but because I never felt fully seen.

Looking back, I realize that most of those people were doing the best they could. Many of them probably thought they were helping. Some may have even believed that sharing their own experiences would comfort me. I don't hold resentment toward them. What I carry is frustration over how difficult it can be for people to simply listen. Sometimes understanding isn't about finding similarities. Sometimes understanding begins by admitting that you don't fully understand at all. Sometimes the most comforting words aren't "I know exactly what you're going through." Sometimes the most comforting words are, "Tell me more."

The truth is, I wasn't angry because people related to me. I was angry because they stopped listening to me. In a season of my life when I desperately needed to feel heard, every assumption felt like another closed door. Every "I know exactly how you feel" felt like another reminder that my voice wasn't reaching the people around me. More than anything, I wanted someone to hear the whole story before deciding they already knew how it ended.

***Part II:* Don't downplay.**

I knew that stress was normal. I knew that nervousness was normal. I knew that everyone had bad days, difficult moments, and periods of uncertainty. I was never asking for the world to stop spinning because I was struggling. I understood that life came with challenges. What made me angry was when people took something that felt life-altering to me and reduced it to something ordinary. Over and over again, I heard some version of the same message. "Everyone goes through that." "That's just part of life." "You'll be fine." "That's normal." Those words were usually meant to reassure me, but they rarely felt reassuring. Instead, they made me feel smaller. They made me feel as though the pain I was trying so hard to explain was being dismissed before it was ever understood.

What frustrated me most was that people seemed to think

I was talking about everyday worries. They thought I was describing ordinary stress, ordinary fear, ordinary anxiety. They didn't understand that what I was experiencing felt anything but ordinary. There were moments when my mind convinced me something was seriously wrong. Moments when fear consumed every thought. Moments when I felt trapped inside my own head. Yet somehow, after explaining all of that, I would hear someone casually tell me that everyone felt that way sometimes. I remember thinking that if they could spend just one day inside my mind, they would never call it normal again.

The best way I can describe it is this: imagine your arm is falling off. Imagine the pain is obvious, immediate, and impossible to ignore. Imagine trying to explain that pain to someone, only to have them shrug and say, "Everybody gets hurt sometimes." Technically, they wouldn't be wrong. Everyone does get hurt sometimes. But that response completely misses the point. The issue isn't whether pain exists. The issue is the severity of it. The issue is whether the person standing in front of you is actually seeing what you're carrying. That's what those conversations felt like. I wasn't saying life was hard. I was saying something felt deeply wrong. Yet people kept responding as though I was merely inconvenienced.

What made it worse was that the comments often came from people who genuinely cared. They weren't trying to minimize my struggles. They weren't trying to be cruel. They simply couldn't see what I was experiencing. Because my wounds weren't visible, they assumed they couldn't be serious. Because my smile still worked some days, they assumed I must be okay. Because I kept showing up to school, to events, to practices, and to everyday life, they assumed I was functioning normally. What they couldn't see was the battle taking place behind all of that. They couldn't see how much energy it took just to appear okay. They couldn't see how much fear I carried into ordinary moments. They couldn't see the exhaustion that came from fighting thoughts that never seemed to rest.

There were times when being told it was normal made me question myself. Maybe they were right, I thought. Maybe I was overreacting. Maybe I was making something out of nothing. Maybe everyone else felt this way and somehow managed it better than I could. Those thoughts became dangerous because they kept me from trusting my own experience. Instead of seeking understanding, I started questioning whether I deserved it. Instead of recognizing that I needed help, I started wondering whether I was simply weak. Looking back, I realize how unfair that was to myself. I was comparing my reality to other people's assumptions.

The truth is, I wasn't looking for someone to tell me I was special. I wasn't looking for people to treat me differently. I wasn't asking anyone to pretend my struggles were unique. I was simply asking people to acknowledge that what I was experiencing was real. There is a difference between saying, "You're not alone," and saying, "That's normal." One statement offers comfort. The other can feel dismissive. One tells someone that others have survived similar battles. The other risks making them feel guilty for struggling in the first place.

What made me angry wasn't the phrase itself. It was what the phrase communicated. Every time someone told me it was normal, I felt as though they were asking me to lower the volume on my pain so it would fit inside their understanding of the world. They wanted my experience to make sense to them. They wanted it to fit neatly into a category they recognized. But my reality didn't feel neat. It didn't feel manageable. It didn't feel normal. It felt overwhelming. It felt frightening. It felt like I was fighting something I couldn't fully explain.

The truth is, I knew life wasn't supposed to be easy. I knew everyone carried burdens I couldn't see. But I also knew that what I was experiencing deserved more than a shrug and a cliché. I didn't need someone to tell me everything would be okay. I didn't need someone to explain away my fears. I needed someone willing to acknowledge that what I was carrying was heavy. Sometimes the most painful part of struggling isn't the struggle itself. Sometimes it's watching people reduce your pain to something ordinary when it feels anything but.

***Part III:* Believe it or not.**

Being misunderstood hurt. Being dismissed hurt. Being told that what I was experiencing was normal hurt. But nothing made me angrier than feeling like people didn't believe me at all.

Some people never said the words directly. They didn't have to. Disbelief has a way of showing itself without ever being spoken aloud. It appeared in the raised eyebrows, the skeptical looks, the awkward silences, and the comments that seemed harmless on the surface but carried a deeper message underneath. "You're probably just stressed." "You think too much." "You're being dramatic." "You just need to relax." Sometimes the words changed, but the message stayed the same: whatever was happening to me couldn't possibly be as serious as I claimed it was.

That anger didn't come from wanting sympathy. It didn't come from wanting attention. If anything, attention was often the last thing I wanted. The anger came from feeling invisible. I was fighting a battle every single day, and it felt like some people were standing on the sidelines insisting there wasn't a war happening at all. Imagine trying to explain a fire while everyone around you argues about whether they can see smoke. Imagine trying to convince people you're drowning while they're busy explaining why the water isn't that deep. That's what it felt like. The problem wasn't just the struggle itself. The problem was having to prove that the struggle existed.

What many people don't understand about mental health is that disbelief creates a second burden. The first burden is the actual pain. The second burden is convincing people the pain is real. There were days when I felt like I spent more energy explaining my struggles than surviving them. Instead of focusing on getting better, I found myself defending my reality. Instead of seeking support, I found myself gathering evidence. I became trapped in an exhausting cycle where I felt responsible for making other people understand something they had never experienced themselves.

The worst part was what happened after hearing those messages enough times. Eventually, their voices started sounding like my own. Every time someone suggested I was overreacting, a small part of me wondered if they were right. Every time someone implied I was being dramatic, I questioned myself. Every time someone dismissed my experience, I became a little less confident in my own understanding of what I was feeling. The disbelief around me slowly became self-doubt within me.

That is one of the cruelest things about not being believed. It doesn't just affect how other people see you. It affects how you see yourself. When enough people question your reality, you start questioning it too. You start wondering if maybe you're exaggerating. Maybe you're weak. Maybe you're making a bigger deal out of things than you should. Maybe everyone else is right and you're wrong. Those thoughts can be incredibly dangerous because they make it harder to ask for help. After all, if you're constantly being told that your struggle isn't real, eventually you start wondering whether you deserve help in the first place.

What made me angry wasn't just that people doubted me. It was what their doubt implied. It suggested that my pain needed permission to exist. It suggested that my experience wasn't valid unless someone else approved it. It suggested that because my wounds couldn't be seen, they somehow mattered less. Nobody asks someone with a broken leg to prove they're injured. Nobody tells someone with a visible wound that they're probably exaggerating. Yet when the injury exists inside your mind, people suddenly become experts. They suddenly feel qualified to decide whether your pain is real enough, serious enough, or worthy enough of attention.

There were moments when I felt completely unhelpable. Not because help didn't exist, but because you can't help something that nobody believes needs help. That's the part that still stays with me. The feeling that before I could even begin healing, I first had to convince people there was something to heal from. I had to argue for my own reality. I had to justify my own pain. I had to explain why I couldn't simply move on, get over it, or think differently.

Looking back, I understand that some people doubted me because they didn't know what else to do. Some doubted me because they were uncomfortable. Some doubted me because accepting my reality would have forced them to confront realities they didn't understand. But understanding their reasons doesn't erase the impact. It doesn't erase the loneliness that came from feeling unseen. It doesn't erase the frustration of speaking honestly and feeling like your words are being weighed against someone else's assumptions.

The truth is, I wasn't angry because people had questions. I wasn't angry because they lacked answers. I was angry because I knew what I was living through, and some people acted as though they knew my reality better than I did. They looked at my life from the outside and made conclusions about battles they couldn't see. They decided what was real and what wasn't. They decided what deserved concern and what didn't.

And in doing so, they taught me one of the hardest lessons of my journey: sometimes the people who need help the most are the people who spend the most time trying to prove they need it at all.

Part IV: Mad at mind.

There came a point when I stopped being angry at other people and started being angry at myself—or at least, what felt like myself. Because after the comments, the misunderstandings, and the disbelief faded into the background, there was still one thing I couldn't escape: my own mind.

That was the part that made me the angriest.

I could walk away from people. I could end conversations. I could leave a room. I could ignore a text message. But I couldn't walk away from my thoughts. No matter where I went, they followed. No matter how hard I tried to distract myself, they found me. They sat beside me in classrooms. They followed me into restaurants. They climbed into the passenger seat of my car. They laid beside me in bed. They showed up during the happiest moments of my life and somehow convinced me that something was wrong.

For a long time, I kept asking myself the same question.

Why are you doing this to me?

Not to another person.

Not to anxiety.

Not to the world.

To my own mind.

The very thing that was supposed to protect me felt like it had turned against me. My mind was supposed to help me recognize danger, not create it. It was supposed to bring me peace, not constantly search for reasons to panic. It was supposed to be my greatest ally. Instead, it often felt like my greatest obstacle.

That realization filled me with anger because I didn't know where to direct it. When someone hurts you, you know who to blame. When circumstances disappoint you, you know what to blame. But what do you do when the thing hurting you is your own mind? What do you do when the enemy knows every weakness you have because it lives inside you?

There were days when I felt betrayed by my own thoughts. Good things would happen, and instead of enjoying them, my mind would find something to worry about. I could be surrounded by people I loved and still feel fear creeping into the moment. I could achieve something I had worked hard for and immediately begin worrying about losing it. It felt like my mind had become incapable of leaving well enough alone. Every moment of peace was questioned. Every moment of happiness was inspected. Every moment of calm felt temporary.

I became angry at the constant worrying. Angry at the

fear that appeared without invitation. Angry at the intrusive thoughts that seemed to arrive at the worst possible times. Angry at the panic that convinced my body something was wrong even when everything around me was perfectly fine. Angry at the fact that I knew some of these thoughts didn't make sense and yet still felt powerless to stop them. There is a unique frustration that comes from recognizing a lie while your body reacts as though it is the truth. It's like watching a fire alarm go off in a building that isn't burning. You know there isn't a fire, but the alarm keeps screaming anyway.

That was one of the hardest parts. People often assume that anxiety is simply worrying too much. They imagine that if you could just think differently, everything would be fine. But many times, I already knew my fears weren't rational. Logic wasn't the problem. Knowledge wasn't the problem. The problem was that my body and mind often refused to listen to logic. I could tell myself I was safe. I could remind myself that I was okay. I could repeat every reassuring thought imaginable. Yet fear would still sit there, stubborn and unrelenting, refusing to leave.

And I hated that.

I hated feeling trapped inside my own head. I hated feeling like I couldn't trust the very thing that was supposed to guide me through life. I hated second-guessing myself. I hated questioning thoughts, feelings, sensations, and experiences that other people seemed to navigate effortlessly. Most of all, I hated feeling like I was losing a battle against something I couldn't physically see.

There were moments when I became exhausted from fighting. Not because I wanted to give up, but because I wanted a break. I wanted one day where my mind wasn't searching for problems. One day where I could experience life without analyzing every feeling. One day where I could wake up and simply exist without immediately preparing for a battle that hadn't even started yet. What angered me most was that those requests felt so small. I wasn't asking for perfection. I wasn't asking for a flawless life. I was asking for quiet.

But quiet felt impossible.

The truth is, I spent a long time believing my mind was broken. I looked at the way other people seemed to move through life and wondered why I couldn't do the same. Why couldn't I just enjoy things? Why couldn't I stop worrying? Why couldn't I let things go? Why couldn't I be normal? Those questions haunted me because I didn't have answers for them. All I had was frustration. Frustration at a mind that seemed determined to make simple things complicated and peaceful moments difficult.

Looking back, I realize that much of that anger came from fear. I was afraid of what my mind might do next. Afraid of how long the struggle would last. Afraid that I would never feel like myself again. But fear has a way of disguising itself. Sometimes it looks like frustration. Sometimes it looks like bitterness. Sometimes it looks like rage. In my case, it often looked like anger directed inward.

The truth is, I wasn't angry because I hated myself. I was angry because I missed myself. I missed the version of me that didn't question every thought. I missed the version of me that could enjoy a moment without wondering what might ruin it. I missed the version of me that trusted his own mind. More than anything, I was angry because the place that should have felt safest—my own head—had become the place where I felt most trapped.

And there is no anger quite like the anger of wanting to escape somewhere you can never leave.

Part V: Angry at anxiety.

There were times when I stopped being angry at people. There were times when I stopped being angry at my own mind. Eventually, all of that anger found a new target: anxiety itself.

If anxiety were a person, I would have a lot to say to it.

I would ask why it showed up uninvited and refused to leave. I would ask why it took ordinary moments and filled them with fear. I would ask why it turned simple tasks into challenges and peaceful moments into battlegrounds. Most of all, I would ask why it stole so much joy from my life.

Because that's what hurts the most.

Not the panic attacks.

Not the doctor's appointments.

Not the sleepless nights.

Not even the fear.

What hurts the most is the joy that disappeared along the way.

People often think anxiety only affects the bad moments. They imagine it appears during stressful situations, creates problems, and then goes away. That wasn't my experience. Anxiety had a way of reaching into the good moments too. It had a way of taking things I loved and covering them with uncertainty. It had a way of showing up when I was supposed to be happy and reminding me that happiness never felt completely safe.

There were moments in my life that should have been simple. Moments that should have existed without fear attached to them. Moments that should have become memories untouched by worry. Instead, anxiety found its way into those moments and claimed space it never deserved.

That's what made me angry.

I wasn't angry because life was difficult. Everyone experiences difficult seasons. I was angry because anxiety seemed determined to follow me into the moments that were supposed to provide relief. It wasn't satisfied with stealing peace. It wanted joy too.

There is a difference between happiness and joy. Happiness is often temporary. It comes and goes. Joy is deeper. Joy is the ability to experience life without constantly looking over your shoulder. Joy is feeling present in a moment instead of fearing what comes next. Joy is trusting yourself enough to enjoy something without immediately preparing for disaster.

Anxiety robbed me of that.

It made every good moment feel fragile. It made every calm day feel temporary. It made every victory feel vulnerable. Instead of enjoying the present, I found myself bracing for the future. Instead of appreciating what was happening, I worried about what might happen. Instead of living in the moment, I constantly felt pulled out of it.

That is an exhausting way to live.

The worst part is that anxiety rarely announces itself honestly. It doesn't walk into the room and say, "I'm here to steal your joy." It disguises itself as caution. It disguises itself as preparation. It disguises itself as responsibility. It convinces you that worrying is helping. It convinces you that fear is protecting you. It convinces you that constantly preparing for the worst is somehow keeping you safe.

Meanwhile, life keeps moving.

Moments pass.

Memories are made.

Experiences come and go.

And before you realize it, you've spent so much time preparing for life that you've forgotten how to participate in it.

That's what angered me.

There were days when I felt as though anxiety had become a thief. Not a thief that stole money or possessions, but a thief that stole experiences. A thief that stole presence. A thief that stole opportunities to fully enjoy the people, places, and moments around me.

The frustrating part is that from the outside, nothing appeared missing. If someone looked at my life, they would still see achievements. They would still see milestones. They would still see accomplishments. They would still see smiles in photographs. What they couldn't see was how many of those moments were spent fighting battles nobody else knew existed.

What they couldn't see was how often anxiety stood in the background.

Even during good days.

Even during celebrations.

Even during moments that should have felt carefree.

It was always there, waiting for an opportunity to whisper another fear into my ear.

I became angry because anxiety turned life into something that felt conditional. It made joy feel dependent on whether my mind decided to cooperate. It made peace feel temporary. It made calmness feel suspicious. Sometimes if I felt genuinely happy, I immediately wondered why. Sometimes if I felt relaxed, I started waiting for something bad to happen. It was as though anxiety had convinced me that joy was dangerous because joy could be lost.

Nobody talks enough about that part.

People talk about fear.

People talk about sadness.

People talk about panic.

But they don't always talk about the grief that comes from realizing how much joy anxiety has taken from you.

Not because it stole every happy moment.

But because it stole pieces of so many of them.

The truth is, I don't hate anxiety because it made me scared. I hate anxiety because it made me doubt my ability to enjoy life. I hate anxiety because it convinced me to spend precious moments worrying instead of living. I hate anxiety because it sat in places where it didn't belong and demanded attention it never deserved.

Most of all, I hate anxiety because it took something from me that I can never fully get back.

It took time.

It took peace.

It took confidence.

But above everything else, it took joy.

And there are few losses more painful than realizing that something invisible has been quietly stealing pieces of your happiness for years while you desperately try to hold on to what remains.

***Part VI:* Waiting room.**

I could handle a lot of things. I could handle bad days. I could handle difficult conversations. I could handle doctor's appointments. I could handle therapy. I could even handle fear. What I struggled to handle was the waiting.

The waiting was its own kind of pain.

At first, I thought the hardest part of my mental health journey would be finding answers. Then I thought the hardest part would be accepting those answers. Eventually, I realized the hardest part was living in the space between questions and solutions. It was waking up every day not knowing whether things would improve, stay the same, or get worse. It was existing in a constant state of uncertainty while everyone around me continued living their lives.

People talk about recovery as if it's a straight line. They talk about getting help, finding treatment, doing the work, and getting better. What they rarely talk about is how much waiting exists between those steps. Waiting for appointments. Waiting for test results. Waiting for medication to work. Waiting for therapy to help. Waiting for answers. Waiting for relief. Waiting for some sign that all of the effort was leading somewhere.

I became angry because my life often felt paused while I waited for something to change.

There is a unique frustration that comes from knowing you're trying everything you can and still having no guarantee that it will work. Every appointment carried hope. Every medication carried hope. Every conversation carried hope. But hope is a dangerous thing when it repeatedly collides with uncertainty. Every time I allowed myself to believe something might finally help, I also opened myself up to disappointment.

That cycle became exhausting.

Something new would begin.

I would feel hopeful.

I would wait.

Nothing would happen.

Then the process would start all over again.

Another appointment.

Another recommendation.

Another possibility.

Another period of waiting.

There were moments when I felt like my entire life had become a waiting room. Not just the literal waiting rooms in doctor's offices, but the emotional waiting room I carried everywhere. I was constantly waiting for the next answer, the next breakthrough, the next piece of information that might explain why I felt the way I did. While other people were planning their futures, I was often focused on making it through the next day.

That made me angry.

Not because I expected immediate solutions. I understood that healing takes time. I understood that mental health isn't simple. What angered me was the uncertainty. If someone had told me exactly when things would improve, I could have endured almost anything. If someone had pointed to a date on a calendar and said, "You'll be okay by then," I would have counted down the days.

But nobody could do that.

Nobody knew.

Not the doctors.

Not the therapists.

Not my family.

Not my friends.

And certainly not me.

Every morning felt like opening a book without knowing whether the next chapter would be better or worse than the last. Some days brought progress. Some days brought setbacks. Some days brought nothing at all. The unpredictability made it difficult to trust the process because I couldn't see where the process was leading.

I often felt trapped between hope and frustration. Hope told me to keep going. Frustration asked how much longer I was supposed to wait. Hope told me healing was possible. Frustration reminded me how long I had already been fighting. Hope encouraged patience. Frustration demanded results.

Those two voices argued constantly.

Some days hope won.

Other days frustration did.

What people don't always understand is that waiting can become exhausting even when you're moving forward. Progress doesn't always feel like progress when it happens slowly. Sometimes change is so gradual that you don't notice it. Sometimes growth happens in increments too small to celebrate. Sometimes you're improving while still feeling miserable.

That was one of the hardest realities for me to accept.

I wanted certainty.

I wanted answers.

I wanted proof.

Instead, I got patience.

And patience was not something I wanted to learn.

I became angry because it felt unfair that so much of my life was spent waiting. Waiting while other people seemed free to simply live. Waiting while memories were being made. Waiting while milestones came and went. Waiting while time continued moving forward whether I felt ready or not.

Looking back, I realize that much of my anger came from the feeling that life was happening without me. While everyone else appeared to be moving forward, I felt stuck.

While everyone else seemed focused on the future, I felt trapped in the present. While everyone else was building their lives, I was waiting for mine to feel manageable again.

The truth is, I wasn't angry because healing took time. I was angry because nobody could tell me how much time it would take. I was angry because uncertainty became a permanent companion. I was angry because every answer seemed to create new questions. I was angry because so many moments of my life felt suspended between where I was and where I wanted to be.

Most of all, I was angry because I kept believing relief was just around the corner, only to find another corner waiting for me.

And after enough corners, after enough waiting rooms, after enough unanswered questions, the waiting itself became a burden.

Not as heavy as the struggle.

But heavy enough to carry every single day.

***Part VII:* What I lost.**

Anxiety didn't just take my peace.

It took me.

Or at least, that's what it felt like.

When people talk about loss, they usually talk about things they can point to. They talk about opportunities missed, relationships that ended, time that can never be recovered, or experiences that slipped away. Those losses are real. I experienced some of them myself. But the loss that hurt me the most wasn't something I could hold in my hands. It wasn't a moment. It wasn't an event. It wasn't even a year of my life.

It was my sense of self.

Somewhere between the fear, the appointments, the uncertainty, the waiting, the overthinking, and the endless battle happening inside my head, I stopped recognizing myself.

That realization terrified me.

Before my mental health struggles became the center of my life, I never spent much time thinking about who I was. I simply existed. I laughed when things were funny. I looked forward to events. I made plans without questioning every possible outcome. I experienced life without constantly monitoring my own thoughts. I wasn't perfect. Nobody is. But I felt like myself.

Then something changed.

Slowly, almost without noticing it, I began measuring life differently. Every decision became filtered through fear. Every experience became analyzed. Every feeling became something to investigate. Instead of simply living, I found myself managing. Managing thoughts. Managing worries. Managing emotions. Managing possibilities. Managing fears that often hadn't even happened.

And eventually I started wondering where the real me had gone.

That's what made me angry.

Not because I had changed.

People change all the time.

Not because I had grown.

Growth is a natural part of life.

I was angry because it felt like I hadn't chosen the change. It felt like my mind had made the decision for me.

I missed the version of myself that existed before every thought felt like a potential threat. I missed the version of myself that didn't spend so much energy fighting invisible battles. I missed the version of myself that trusted his own mind. I missed the version of myself that could enjoy a moment without immediately searching for something that might ruin it.

Most of all, I missed the version of myself that felt free.

There were moments when I looked at old photos and felt like I was looking at someone else. Not because I had physically changed, but because I remembered what life felt like when those pictures were taken. I remembered what it felt like to exist without constantly carrying the weight of anxiety. I remembered what it felt like to simply be present.

And I wanted that version of myself back.

That's a difficult thing to admit.

People often tell you that struggles make you stronger. They tell you that hardships build character. They tell you that challenges shape who you become. Maybe all of those things are true. But sometimes those statements overlook something important.

Sometimes growth comes with grief.

Because while you are becoming someone new, you are also saying goodbye to someone old.

I don't think enough people talk about that.

I grieved the person I thought I was going to be.

I grieved the teenager I imagined becoming.

I grieved the version of my life that I expected to have.

Not because my life was over.

Not because my future disappeared.

But because the path I expected was gone.

The person I expected to be was gone.

And no matter how hard I tried, I couldn't return to the place I had been before.

That made me angry.

I was angry that something invisible had changed the way I experienced the world. I was angry that I couldn't simply flip a switch and go back. I was angry that I spent so much time searching for pieces of myself that felt lost. I was angry that every step forward seemed to come with another reminder of what had been left behind.

The hardest part wasn't losing confidence.

It wasn't losing peace.

It wasn't even losing joy.

The hardest part was losing familiarity.

I no longer felt at home inside myself.

Imagine living in the same house your entire life and suddenly realizing every room feels unfamiliar. The walls are still there. The furniture hasn't moved. The address hasn't changed. Yet somehow everything feels different.

That's what my mind became.

I still looked like me.

I still sounded like me.

I still answered to the same name.

But inside, something felt different.

Something felt missing.

There were days when I wondered whether I would ever fully feel like myself again. Days when I questioned whether the person I remembered was gone forever. Days when I looked ahead and couldn't imagine a future that didn't involve constantly fighting my own thoughts.

Those were painful questions.

And painful questions often become anger when they remain unanswered long enough.

The truth is, I wasn't angry because I lost who I was.

I was angry because I couldn't find him.

I kept searching for the version of me that existed before anxiety became so loud. I kept searching for the person who moved through life without fear controlling every decision. I kept searching for the person I remembered.

But over time, I realized something difficult.

That person wasn't waiting for me.

He wasn't lost.

He wasn't hiding.

He was gone.

Not because anxiety destroyed him.

Not because struggle erased him.

But because life had changed me.

And maybe that's what hurt the most.

The realization that I couldn't go backward.

The realization that I couldn't reclaim every piece of myself that had been altered by the journey.

The realization that some losses don't involve death, yet still require mourning.

The truth is, anxiety didn't just take my peace.

It took my sense of who I was.

And there were days when I would have traded almost anything just to feel like myself again.

***Part VIII:* Myself.**

After a while, I ran out of people to blame.

I had been angry at those who didn't listen. I had been angry at those who minimized my struggles. I had been angry at those who didn't believe me. I had been angry at anxiety. I had been angry at my mind. But eventually, all of that anger found its way back to the person I saw every morning in the mirror.

Me.

Looking back, I think this was the most painful anger of all.

When you're angry at other people, there is distance. You can walk away. You can disagree. You can tell yourself that they simply don't understand. But when you're angry at yourself, there is nowhere to go. The voice follows you everywhere because it lives inside your own head.

For a long time, I became my own harshest critic.

I blamed myself for struggling.

I blamed myself for needing help.

I blamed myself for not getting better fast enough.

I blamed myself for not knowing how to fix things.

I blamed myself for the fear, the panic, the uncertainty, and the disruption that mental health had brought into my life.

The accusations never seemed to stop.

Why can't you handle this?

Why are you like this?

Why can't you just move on?

Why can't you think normally?

Why does everything feel so difficult?

Why did you let it get this bad?

Those questions became a soundtrack that played quietly in the background of my life. Some days it was barely noticeable. Other days it was deafening.

What made it worse was that I genuinely believed I should have been able to control it. I thought strength meant overcoming every challenge on my own. I thought resilience meant never needing help. I thought courage meant solving every problem without letting anyone see me struggle.

So when I found myself sitting in doctor's offices, taking medication, attending appointments, and trying to navigate a mind that felt completely unpredictable, I felt like I had failed some invisible test.

I know now that those beliefs weren't fair.

But at the time, they felt real.

I watched other people go about their lives and wondered what was wrong with me. Why did everything seem easier for them? Why could they move through life without constantly questioning themselves? Why could they trust their thoughts while I felt trapped by mine?

The comparison was relentless.

And comparison is dangerous because it rarely tells the full story.

I compared my worst moments to other people's best moments.

I compared my private battles to their public appearances.

I compared my struggles to assumptions.

And every comparison left me feeling smaller.

There were days when I convinced myself that I was the problem. Not anxiety. Not fear. Not mental health. Me.

I thought maybe I was weak.

Maybe I wasn't trying hard enough.

Maybe everyone else was right.

Maybe I was overreacting.

Maybe I should just get over it.

The frightening thing about self-blame is how convincing it can become. The longer you hear something, the easier it is to believe. And after hearing enough dismissive comments, enough misunderstandings, and enough doubts, I began repeating those same messages to myself.

I became the very person I needed protection from.

That's something I wish more people understood about

mental health. Sometimes the loudest criticism doesn't come from outside voices. Sometimes it comes from within. Sometimes the person judging you most harshly isn't a stranger, a friend, or a teacher.

It's you.

I held myself responsible for things that were never mine to control. I expected myself to have answers I didn't possess. I demanded perfection during a season of life that was already difficult enough. I acted as though struggling was a personal failure instead of a human experience.

And when I couldn't meet those impossible standards, I became angry.

Angry that I wasn't stronger.

Angry that I wasn't recovering faster.

Angry that I couldn't think my way out of the problem.

Angry that I needed support.

Angry that I couldn't return to the person I used to be.

But beneath all of that anger was something else.

Fear.

I was afraid that maybe this was who I would always be.

Afraid that things would never improve.

Afraid that the version of myself I remembered was gone forever.

Afraid that everyone else's doubts might somehow be true.

It's easier to be angry than it is to admit you're scared.

Anger feels powerful.

Fear feels vulnerable.

So I chose anger.

I directed it toward myself because I didn't know where else to put it.

The truth is, I spoke to myself in ways I would never speak

to another person. I said things to myself that I would never say to a friend who was struggling. I demanded things from myself that I would never demand from someone I cared about. I expected perfection while offering myself no grace.

That's one of the saddest realizations I've had.

If someone I loved had been carrying the same burdens I was carrying, I would have shown them compassion. I would have reminded them that healing takes time. I would have encouraged them to keep going. I would have told them that their struggles didn't define their worth.

Yet somehow I couldn't offer those same words to myself.

Instead, I became my own prosecutor.

Every setback became evidence.

Every bad day became proof.

Every difficult moment became another reason to blame myself.

And the trial never ended.

The truth is, I wasn't angry because I hated myself.

I was angry because I couldn't understand myself.

I couldn't understand why my mind felt the way it did.

I couldn't understand why life had become so difficult.

I couldn't understand why I was carrying a weight that seemed invisible to everyone else.

So I looked for someone to blame.

Eventually, that someone became me.

Looking back now, I realize something important. The person I blamed the most was actually the person fighting the hardest. The version of me I criticized every day was waking up and continuing despite fear. He was showing up despite uncertainty. He was surviving despite exhaustion.

He wasn't failing.

He was fighting.

But at the time, I couldn't see that.

All I could see was someone who wasn't who he used to be.

And I hated him for it.

The truth is, some of the deepest wounds from my mental health journey weren't caused by anxiety, fear, or panic.

They were caused by the way I treated myself while I was struggling.

And for a long time, that was the anger I carried the heaviest.

Part IX: Angry at Silence.

I was surrounded by people.

Friends.

Family.

Classmates.

Teammates.

Teachers.

Doctors.

Therapists.

At almost every point in my journey, there were people around me. There were people who cared. People who wanted to help. People who wanted me to get better.

Yet some of the loneliest moments of my life happened in rooms full of people.

That's what made me angry.

Not because I was abandoned.

Not because nobody cared.

But because no matter how many people stood around me, nobody could climb inside my mind and see what was happening.

There is a loneliness that comes from being physically alone.

But there is a different kind of loneliness that comes from being surrounded by people and still feeling completely unseen.

That's the loneliness I carried.

The hardest part wasn't that I had no one to talk to. The hardest part was that I didn't know how to explain what was happening. How do you describe thoughts that don't make sense? How do you explain fears that feel real but sound irrational when spoken aloud? How do you communicate a battle that nobody else can see?

I didn't know.

Most days, I barely understood it myself.

People would ask how I was doing, and I would give the answer everyone expected.

"I'm fine."

"I'm okay."

"Just tired."

"Just stressed."

The truth was almost always more complicated than that.

But explaining it felt impossible.

Not because I wanted to hide it.

Because I didn't have the words.

Sometimes I would sit there trying to describe what I was feeling and realize that every explanation sounded inadequate. The fear was bigger than the language I had available to describe it. The thoughts were louder than the words I could find. The struggle was deeper than any simple answer could capture.

So instead of explaining it, I often carried it.

Alone.

That silence became heavy.

People often assume silence means nothing is happening. They assume that if someone isn't talking about their pain, the pain must not be there. But silence can be incredibly loud. Sometimes silence is filled with fear. Sometimes silence is filled with confusion. Sometimes silence is filled with questions that nobody seems capable of answering.

For me, silence was filled with all three.

I carried conversations inside my head that never reached the outside world. Questions I never asked. Fears I never fully explained. Thoughts I never completely shared. Not because I didn't want help, but because I didn't know how to hand someone a struggle I couldn't fully understand myself.

That made me angry.

I watched people communicate things that seemed simple. They could explain a bad day. They could explain disappointment. They could explain stress. Meanwhile, I was trying to explain something that felt invisible, unpredictable, and overwhelming all at once.

It felt like speaking a language nobody else understood.

Imagine standing in a crowded room, desperately trying to explain something important, only to realize that every word is being translated incorrectly. That's what many conversations felt like. People heard me, but they didn't always understand me. And sometimes I wasn't even sure I understood myself.

The isolation that came from that was difficult to describe.

I could be laughing with friends and still feel alone.

I could be sitting with family and still feel alone.

I could be surrounded by support and still feel alone.

Not because those people failed me.

Because there were parts of my experience that never

seemed to make the journey from my mind to someone else's understanding.

That gap became one of the loneliest places I have ever lived.

There were moments when I wondered whether anyone would ever truly understand. Moments when I felt trapped inside my own experience. Moments when I wanted desperately for someone to see exactly what was happening without requiring me to explain it.

I wanted someone to understand without translation.

Without simplification.

Without assumptions.

Without comparison.

I wanted someone to see the entire picture.

But life doesn't work that way.

People can support you.

People can love you.

People can listen to you.

But nobody can completely live inside your experience.

Realizing that was painful.

And for a long time, it made me angry.

I was angry that my struggle felt so difficult to explain. Angry that words constantly seemed inadequate. Angry that some thoughts felt too complicated to describe and too loud to ignore. Angry that I could spend hours trying to explain my experience and still walk away feeling misunderstood.

Most of all, I was angry because the silence often convinced me I was alone.

Not physically.

Emotionally.

Mentally.

Internally.

The silence made it easy to believe that nobody else could possibly understand. It made it easy to believe that I was carrying something unique, isolated, and impossible to share.

Looking back, I know that wasn't entirely true. There were people who cared. There were people who listened. There were people who tried. But when you're trapped inside your own mind, effort doesn't always erase loneliness.

Sometimes the loneliness remains.

Sometimes the silence remains.

Sometimes the questions remain.

The truth is, one of the hardest parts of my mental health journey wasn't the fear itself.

It wasn't the panic.

It wasn't even the uncertainty.

It was the feeling that I was carrying all of it inside a mind that nobody else could enter.

A war that nobody else could see.

A language nobody else could fully speak.

A silence that nobody else could fully hear.

And for a long time, that silence was louder than anything else in my life.

***Part X:* Angry that I survived.**

I never wanted to become strong.

I know that sounds strange. People celebrate strength. They admire resilience. They praise perseverance. They tell stories about overcoming adversity and finding courage in the middle of hardship. Strength is treated like a trophy. Something to be proud of. Something to aspire toward.

But if I'm being honest, I never wanted the circumstances that required it.

I didn't want to become resilient.

I wanted to be a teenager.

I didn't want to learn how to survive.

I wanted to learn how to live.

That's what made me angry.

For years, people told me that these were supposed to be the best years of my life. The years filled with freedom, friendships, memories, laughter, and discovery. The years I would someday look back on with nostalgia. The years everyone says you'll miss when they're gone.

And maybe for some people, that's true.

But for me, those years often felt like something entirely different.

While other people were making memories, I was making appointments.

While other people were planning weekends, I was planning around anxiety.

While other people were enjoying the present, I was trying to survive it.

While other people were discovering who they were, I felt like I was losing who I was.

That reality made me angry because it felt unfair.

Not unfair in the childish sense of the word. Not the kind of unfairness that comes from losing a game or missing out on something you wanted. This was deeper than that. It was the realization that some of the years I had been told would be the most liberating years of my life felt anything but liberating.

They felt like a cage.

A cage built by fear.

A cage built by uncertainty.

A cage built by a mind that seemed determined to fight me every step of the way.

There were moments when I looked around and wondered why everyone else seemed to be moving forward while I felt stuck. People were creating memories that would last a lifetime. They were enjoying milestones, making plans, and embracing opportunities. Meanwhile, I was spending so much energy trying to feel okay that I often didn't have energy left for anything else.

I wasn't jealous of them.

That's important.

I wasn't angry that other people were happy.

I was grieving the life I thought I was supposed to have.

I was grieving the version of my teenage years I imagined when I was younger. The version where anxiety wasn't sitting in the passenger seat. The version where fear didn't have a voice. The version where my biggest concerns were ordinary teenage concerns instead of constant battles happening inside my own mind.

That's a difficult thing to admit because grief is often associated with losing something that once existed. But I think you can grieve things that never happened too.

You can grieve opportunities.

You can grieve expectations.

You can grieve versions of your life that you never got to experience.

And I did.

I grieved birthdays that felt overshadowed by fear.

I grieved moments that should have felt exciting but instead felt exhausting.

I grieved time that disappeared while I was busy fighting battles nobody else could see.

Most of all, I grieved the years themselves.

Because no matter how much healing happens, there are some things you can't get back.

You can't get back a Tuesday from three years ago.

You can't get back a missed opportunity.

You can't get back moments that were spent surviving when they could have been spent living.

Time only moves in one direction.

That realization hurt.

There were days when I became angry simply because the clock refused to stop. Life kept moving whether I felt ready or not. School continued. Events continued. Milestones continued. The world never paused to give me time to catch my breath.

And sometimes that felt cruel.

People often say that struggles make you stronger.

Maybe they do.

But strength has a cost.

Nobody talks enough about that part.

Nobody talks about the time strength requires.

The experiences strength demands.

The sacrifices strength collects.

The pieces of yourself you lose while earning it.

People see the finished product.

They see resilience.

They see perseverance.

They see determination.

What they don't always see is the price.

The countless moments spent fighting.

The endless uncertainty.

The exhaustion.

The fear.

The loneliness.

The grief.

The years.

Especially the years.

Because if there's one thing I would ask for back, it wouldn't be perfection.

It wouldn't be a life without challenges.

It wouldn't even be a guarantee that everything would work out.

I would ask for time.

Time spent living instead of surviving.

Time spent enjoying instead of worrying.

Time spent being present instead of preparing for disaster.

Time spent feeling free.

The truth is, I know life was never supposed to be perfect. I know everyone faces battles. I know hardship is part of being human. But there is still a part of me that wishes some of my hardest lessons could have waited. There is still a part of me that wishes survival hadn't become such a defining feature of years that were supposed to be filled with discovery and freedom.

I didn't want strength.

I wanted peace.

I didn't want resilience.

I wanted joy.

I didn't want to become an expert in survival.

I wanted the chance to simply live.

And that's the anger I carried for a long time.

Not anger that I struggled.

Not anger that life was difficult.

Not even anger that anxiety existed.

It was anger that so much of my youth was spent learning how to survive while everyone kept telling me these were supposed to be the years when I learned how to live.

But somewhere along the way, I realized something.

The years were not what I expected.

The journey was not what I planned.

The version of myself I imagined becoming never fully arrived.

Yet despite all of that, I am still here.

Not because I was fearless.

Not because I was perfect.

Not because I always believed things would get better.

I am here because I kept going.

Even when I was angry.

Even when I was exhausted.

Even when I felt lost.

Even when I felt robbed of time I could never get back.

I kept going.

The truth is, I never wanted to become strong.

But strength found me anyway.

And while I will always wish some of those years had been different, I can finally admit something I couldn't admit before.

The person who survived them is someone worth being proud of.

Maybe that's the truth I spent all these pages trying to understand. I wasn't angry that I survived. I was angry about what survival cost me. The years, the peace, the certainty, the version of myself I thought I was supposed to become. I was angry because while everyone else seemed to be living, I was learning how to endure. But anger, like fear, can only carry a person so far. Eventually, I had to decide whether I would spend the rest of my life mourning what was lost or building something with what remained. I cannot change the years behind me. I cannot reclaim every moment anxiety stole. I cannot become the person I would have been had this journey never happened. But I can become the person standing here now. The one who kept going when quitting felt easier. The one who survived days he never thought he would survive. The one who is still writing new chapters. And maybe that is enough. Maybe the greatest act of defiance is not surviving what tried to break you. Maybe it is choosing to live after.

11

What I Learned

There's a kind of truth I didn't understand until I stopped trying to outrun my own mind, and it's that healing doesn't make you invulnerable—it just teaches you how to stay present while you're vulnerable. I used to think strength meant not feeling what I felt so intensely. Not getting overwhelmed. Not having moments where everything inside me felt uncertain or unfamiliar. But that version of strength was never real for me. It was just control disguised as survival.

What I've learned instead is something I've come to believe—that vulnerability isn't weakness, but the place where honesty and courage actually begin. And for a long time, I misunderstood that completely. I thought vulnerability was what happened when I was falling apart. But now I understand it's what happens when I stop pretending I'm not human in order to feel safe.

There are still moments where I struggle internally. Still moments where my mind feels louder than I want it to, where I feel slightly detached or overly aware of myself in a way that used to scare me more than anything. Those moments haven't disappeared. But I don't treat them as evidence that I'm failing anymore. I don't immediately turn them into a story about who I am or what I'm becoming.

They're just moments now.

Not verdicts.

That shift didn't happen all at once. It came from living through enough of those experiences to realize that fear doesn't always tell the truth about what's happening. It amplifies. It distorts. It tries to make everything feel final when it isn't. And I spent a long time believing it without question.

Now I don't.

Not always.

Not perfectly.

But more than before.

There are still ups and downs in how I experience myself. Still days where I feel grounded and days where I feel less grounded. Still times where I have to pause and remind myself that what I'm feeling doesn't need to become something bigger than it is. And I still slip sometimes into old patterns of overthinking, of scanning myself too closely, of trying to find certainty in places where certainty doesn't exist.

But I don't stay there the same way anymore.

That's what I keep coming back to.

Because I used to think change would mean never returning to those states again. Now I understand it more as learning how to move through them without losing myself inside them. How to let them pass without turning them into identity. How to experience discomfort without turning it into collapse.

And in that space, I've had to learn something I didn't

expect—that I can be both strong and still struggling. Both aware and still uncertain. Both growing and still human in the middle of it all.

What I once called "breaking" I now understand as being human in real time, without a script for how it's supposed to feel.

There's a point where you start realizing that the goal was never to become someone who never struggles again, but to become someone who doesn't abandon themselves when they do. That sounds simple when it's written out like that, but living it is something else entirely. Because in the middle of it—when your mind feels unfamiliar, when your perception shifts, when anxiety or dissociation or fear shows up—it doesn't feel philosophical. It feels immediate. It feels like something you have to respond to right now or risk losing control.

And I used to respond every time.

Not because I wanted to, but because I believed I had to.

I believed every internal shift meant something important about my safety, my stability, my future, or my identity. I treated my mind like a system I had to constantly monitor in order to keep it from breaking down. And over time, that level of monitoring became its own kind of pressure. I wasn't just experiencing anxiety—I was constantly watching for it, which made it louder than it sometimes needed to be.

That's something I understand differently now.

There are still moments where my mind becomes more noticeable than I want it to be. Moments where I feel slightly disconnected or too aware of my own thinking. And even now, that can bring a flicker of old fear. A memory of what those feelings used to turn into. But the difference is that it doesn't automatically escalate the same way anymore.

I don't immediately assume I'm losing ground.

I don't immediately assume I'm going backward.

I don't immediately assume the feeling is a warning I have to solve.

Sometimes I just let it exist.

And I keep going anyway.

That "keep going anyway" part is what I never understood before. I thought I needed to feel fully okay first in order to continue living normally. But what I've learned instead is that normal doesn't require perfect internal stability. It requires willingness to stay present even when things aren't perfectly clear inside you.

There are still ups and downs in how I experience everything. Still days where I feel grounded and days where I feel less grounded. Still moments where my mind gets louder and I have to consciously slow myself down instead of reacting to every thought as if it's urgent. And I still slip sometimes into old patterns without realizing it right away.

But I don't stay in them the same way anymore.

That's what I keep noticing.

Not that the patterns are gone, but that they don't hold me the same way they used to. They don't stretch as far. They don't last as long. They don't define everything around them. They're still part of my experience, but they're no longer the entire experience.

And I think that's what I've been learning to carry.

Not the absence of struggle.

But the ability to stay myself inside it.

There are still moments where I catch myself trying to measure whether I'm "doing better" in real time, as if healing is something you can accurately grade while you're inside it. I'll notice a shift in my thoughts or my awareness and instinctively try to assign it meaning—good, bad, progress, setback—like I'm supposed to be tracking myself in a way that gives me certainty. But that approach was part of what kept everything so intense for so long.

Because it turns living into constant evaluation.

And I don't want to live like that anymore.

What I've been learning instead is that experience doesn't always need immediate interpretation. A feeling can exist without becoming a conclusion. A shift in awareness can happen without becoming a story. A moment of discomfort doesn't have to be turned into proof of anything about who I am or where I'm headed.

That's still not natural all the time. It still takes effort to not fall back into old habits of checking and analyzing everything internally. Especially when I'm stressed or tired or overwhelmed, my mind still tries to return to that familiar pattern of scanning for certainty. It still wants answers fast. It still wants control.

But I don't always give it that anymore.

There are still ups and downs. Still days where I feel more grounded and days where I feel less grounded. Still moments where I feel slightly detached from myself, like I'm observing instead of fully participating in my own life. And even though I recognize those moments more quickly now, they can still feel uncomfortable in the moment.

The difference is what happens next.

I don't always escalate it.

I don't always spiral.

I don't always turn it into something bigger than it is.

Sometimes I just continue.

And that "continuing" used to feel impossible to me. I used to think that if I didn't fix the feeling immediately, it would grow. I used to think that ignoring it—or even just not fully engaging with it—was dangerous. But I've learned through experience that most of those moments don't demand urgency the way they feel like they do.

They pass on their own more often than I expected.

And I stay.

Not perfectly. Not effortlessly. But I stay.

And I think that's what I've been learning to carry all along without fully realizing it at the beginning. Not how to eliminate every difficult internal moment, but how to stop abandoning myself inside them.

There are parts of my mind that still feel like they remember how things used to be, even when I'm not actively thinking about it. Not memories in the traditional sense, but patterns. The way attention sharpens inward. The way uncertainty used to immediately become fear. The way a small internal shift could suddenly feel like the beginning of something much larger. That wiring doesn't just disappear, even when you've lived long enough to understand it differently.

It just becomes quieter over time.

And sometimes it only shows up in fragments.

A moment where I feel slightly detached. A moment where my thoughts feel more noticeable than usual. A moment where I become aware of myself in a way that used to spiral quickly into panic. Those moments still happen. But they don't always carry the same weight they used to.

That's what's changed.

Not the presence of those experiences, but the way they

move through me.

There are still ups and downs in how I experience everything. Still days where I feel grounded and days where I feel less grounded. Still moments where my mind gets louder and I have to consciously slow myself down instead of reacting immediately to every thought that shows up. And I still slip sometimes into old habits without noticing right away.

But I recover differently now.

That's the part I can't ignore anymore.

It doesn't take as long to come back. It doesn't take as much time to realize I'm in a loop. It doesn't pull me in as deeply as it used to. And even when I do get caught in it, there's usually a point where I recognize it and step out of it again, instead of staying inside it for hours or letting it define the entire day.

That shift didn't happen all at once. It came from repetition. From living through enough of those moments to see that they don't all lead to the same place. That not every uncomfortable feeling is the start of something worse. That not every internal shift is a warning.

And I've had to slowly unlearn the urgency I used to attach to everything I felt.

Because urgency was what made everything heavier than it needed to be.

Now, I try—when I can—to let things exist for a moment before I decide what they mean. To allow space between feeling and reaction. To not immediately turn every internal experience into something I have to solve. And that space has changed how I move through my own mind.

Not perfectly.

But noticeably.

And I think that's what I've been learning all along in

different forms.

How to stay inside my own experience without turning every moment into a crisis.

How to keep going even when my mind feels uncertain.

How to not disappear when things feel unfamiliar.

And I'm still practicing that, even now.

There's a difference I've started to notice between feeling something and becoming it. Before, those two things were almost the same for me. If I felt detached, I was in danger. If I felt anxious, something was wrong. If my mind felt unfamiliar, I assumed I was slipping into something I wouldn't be able to get out of. There wasn't much separation between the experience itself and what I believed it meant.

Now there's a little space between them.

Not a perfect space.

But enough of one to change things.

There are still moments where I feel slightly outside myself, where my awareness becomes sharper than I want it to be, where my thoughts feel more noticeable than my presence. Those moments still show up. And even when they do, I don't always react the same way anymore. I don't always immediately attach fear to them. I don't always assume they're the start of something bigger.

Sometimes I just notice them.

And continue.

That used to be the part I couldn't imagine doing. Continuing while something inside me felt uncertain. Continuing without fully resolving the feeling first. Continuing without needing total clarity before I moved forward. But I've learned that clarity doesn't always arrive on demand, and waiting for it used to cost me more than I realized.

So I've stopped waiting in the same way.

There are still ups and downs. Still days where I feel more grounded and days where I feel less grounded. Still moments where my mind gets louder and I have to actively slow myself down instead of reacting immediately to everything I think or feel. And I still have moments where I fall back into old patterns without noticing at first.

But they don't hold me as long anymore.

That's the part I keep coming back to.

Not that they stopped happening.

But that they don't stay.

They pass.

And I pass by them.

And I think that's what I've been learning to carry through all of this more than anything else. Not the idea of being untouched by struggle, but the ability to move through it without losing myself inside it. To stay present even when my mind feels uncertain. To not turn every internal shift into a conclusion about who I am.

And I'm still practicing that, even now.

I don't think there's ever going to be a version of my life where my mind is completely silent in the way I once thought it needed to be. I used to imagine peace as the absence of everything uncomfortable—no overthinking, no detachment, no moments of uncertainty. But that idea of peace was always more of a fantasy than something my actual life was going to give me. What I understand now is that peace, for me, has become something different entirely.

It's not silence.

It's stability inside the noise.

There are still moments where my mind feels louder than

I want it to. Still moments where I notice myself too much, where I feel slightly outside my own experience, where my thoughts become more present than the world around me. And even though those moments can still be uncomfortable, they don't automatically define everything anymore. They don't take over the full structure of my day the way they used to.

That's what I keep noticing.

Not the absence of struggle, but the change in how much space it gets to take.

There are still ups and downs. Still days where I feel grounded and days where I feel less grounded. There are still times when I have to remind myself not to follow every thought as if it's urgent or meaningful or dangerous. And I still slip sometimes into old patterns of scanning myself too closely, trying to find certainty in places where certainty doesn't exist.

But I come back now.

That's the difference.

I don't stay lost in it in the same way. I don't build entire narratives around single moments of discomfort anymore. I don't automatically assume that what I feel in one moment is going to define everything that comes after it. I've started to see my mind more as something I move through, not something that decides everything about me.

And that shift didn't come from everything getting easier.

It came from learning I could survive it without reacting the same way every time.

That I could feel something uncomfortable and not disappear into it.

That I could stay present even when I didn't feel perfectly

steady.

And I think that's what I've been learning to carry all along, even when I didn't fully understand it in the beginning.

Not a life without struggle.

But a life where struggle doesn't erase me.

And that's enough for me to keep going.

It's you versus you. You will never lose—always remember that.

I'm still winning;

I'm still here,

12

...

AND YOU ARE TOO.

II

PSYCHOEDUCATION

13

Anger Management

What Is Anger?

Anger is a completely normal, healthy, and universal human emotion. It is not a character flaw, a weakness, or something to be permanently suppressed. Anger is a signal—your mind and body alerting you that something feels *wrong*: a boundary has been crossed, an injustice has occurred, you feel threatened, or an important need has gone unmet.

The problem is never anger itself. The problem is **what we do with it**. Anger becomes destructive only when it is expressed in ways that harm ourselves or others, or when it is chronically suppressed to the point where it festers into resentment, depression, or physical illness.

The Signal

"Anger is like a check engine light on a dashboard. It doesn't mean the car is broken—it means something needs attention."

The Anger Iceberg

What people see on the surface is rage, aggression, or coldness. But underneath anger, there is almost always something more vulnerable: **fear, hurt, embarrassment, shame, loneliness, or grief**. Anger is easier to feel than vulnerability because it gives us a sense of power and control.

Example

Marcus snaps at his partner when dinner isn't ready. On the surface: anger. Underneath: fear that he isn't loved, exhaustion from work, and shame that he can't control his environment.

The Physiology of Anger

When anger is triggered, your brain's amygdala (the alarm system) fires before your prefrontal cortex (the reasoning brain) can respond. This is why we say or do things "in the heat of the moment" that we later regret. Stress hormones—adrenaline and cortisol—flood the body, causing:

- Increased heart rate and blood pressure
- Muscle tension (especially in jaw, neck, shoulders)
- Rapid, shallow breathing
- Tunnel vision and reduced problem-solving ability
- The urge to fight, flee, or freeze

Research shows it takes approximately **20–30 minutes** for the body to fully return to its baseline once anger is triggered. This is why "cooling off" genuinely works on a biological level.

Healthy vs. Unhealthy Expression

× *Unhealthy Expression*

- Shouting, screaming, name-calling
- Physical aggression (hitting, throwing)
- Silent treatment / stonewalling
- Passive-aggression (sarcasm, eye-rolling)
- Venting to everyone except the source
- Suppression / bottling it up
- Substance use to numb the feeling
- Self-harm or reckless behavior

✓ *Healthy Expression*

- Naming the feeling: "I'm really angry right now"
- Taking a structured time-out (20+ mins)
- Physical exercise to discharge the energy
- Journaling what triggered you and why
- Using "I" statements to communicate the need
- Identifying the fear or hurt underneath
- Problem-solving once calm
- Therapy or anger management groups

Key Skills for Anger Regulation

1. The STOP Technique

- **S**—Stop. Do not react immediately.
- **T**—Take a breath. Slow, deep diaphragmatic breathing.
- **O**—Observe. What is happening in your body? What

triggered this?
- **P**—Proceed mindfully. Choose a response rather than react impulsively.

2. Opposite Action (DBT)

When anger urges you to yell, withdraw, or escalate—do the opposite. If anger says "push away," try moving closer with curiosity. If anger says "attack," try speaking softly and asking a question.

3. The Time-Out Protocol

Agree ahead of time (ideally when calm) with people in your life that when either person calls "time-out," both parties will separate for at least 20 minutes. During this time: do NOT ruminate on grievances. Instead: breathe, walk, or do something physical. Reconnect when both are regulated.

4. The Anger Log

Keep a daily log for two weeks tracking: What triggered the anger? What were you feeling underneath? How did you respond? What would you do differently? This builds self-awareness and reveals patterns.

Real-Life Example

Sarah gets cut off in traffic and her immediate urge is to honk and yell. Instead, she takes three slow breaths and says out loud: "They probably didn't see me. I'm also stressed because I'm late. I'll take the next exit and take a moment." She arrives still functional rather than escalated for hours.

How to Monitor & Measure Your Progress

1. **Keep a weekly anger log**— rate intensity (1–10), note triggers, note your response, and what you would do differently. Watch average intensity decrease over weeks.
2. **Track "regrettable incidents"**— times you acted on anger in a way you wish you hadn't. Aim for fewer each week.
3. **Notice your early warning signs**— jaw tension, a hot face, hands clenching. The earlier you catch anger, the easier it is to regulate.
4. **Rate your recovery time**— how long does it take to return to baseline? Progress looks like shorter recovery times.
5. **Ask for feedback**— from someone you trust: "Have you noticed any changes in how I handle frustration?"

14

Healthy Relationships

What Makes a Relationship Healthy?

A healthy relationship is not one that is perfect or conflict-free. It is one where both people feel **safe, valued, heard, and free to be themselves**. All relationships—romantic, familial, friendships, professional—exist on a spectrum from healthy to toxic. Understanding the characteristics of a healthy relationship is the first step toward building and maintaining them.

John Gottman's decades of research on couples found that healthy relationships are characterized not by the absence of conflict, but by a ratio of approximately **5 positive interactions for every 1 negative one** (the "Magic Ratio"). This is the balance that predicts long-term relational health.

The 10 Pillars of a Healthy Relationship

1. Mutual Respect

Both people honor each other's feelings, opinions, boundaries, and individuality—even in disagreement. Respect means you do not demean, belittle, or dismiss your partner's perspective, even when you find it frustrating.

Example

"I completely disagree with your decision, but I respect your right to make it and I'm here to support you."

2. Trust & Honesty

Both people feel confident in each other's words and intentions. They are transparent, follow through on commitments, and are willing to have difficult conversations rather than hide the truth. Trust is built in small moments consistently over time.

3. Open Communication

Both people can express needs, feelings, and concerns without fear of punishment, ridicule, or abandonment. This includes the ability to say "I'm upset," "I need space," "I'm not comfortable with that," and to know those statements will be received with care.

4. Individuality & Autonomy

Healthy relationships celebrate each person's individual interests, friendships, values, and identity. You do not need to share every hobby or opinion. You are two whole individuals choosing to be in relationship, not two halves merged into one.

5. Healthy Conflict Resolution

Conflict is normal and even necessary in healthy relationships—it is how we discover differences and negotiate needs. Healthy couples fight *about the issue*, not against each other. They avoid the "Four Horsemen" (Gottman): Criticism, Contempt, Defensiveness, and Stonewalling.

6. Equality & Fairness

Power is shared. Decisions are made together. Neither person uses money, sex, guilt, or fear to control the other. Both people's needs, time, and energy are treated as equally important.

7. Support & Encouragement

Both people actively want to see the other succeed and grow. They celebrate wins, provide comfort in difficult times, and encourage each other's goals—even when those goals require sacrifice or change.

8. Safety

Both people feel emotionally, physically, and psychologically safe. There is no fear of retaliation for expressing honest feelings. Mistakes are handled with grace, not punishment.

9. Accountability

Both people take responsibility for their own behavior. When they hurt the other, they apologize genuinely, seek to understand the impact, and make changes. There is no chronic blame-shifting or deflection.

10. Reciprocity

The giving and taking feels balanced over time. While it will not be perfectly equal day-to-day, both people notice if the relationship is consistently one-sided and address it openly.

How to Monitor & Build Healthier Relationships

1. **Relationship inventory**— For each significant relationship in your life, rate it 1–10 on each of the 10 pillars above. Notice where the gaps are.
2. **Practice one pillar per week**— Focus intentionally on improving one area (e.g., this week I will validate before problem-solving).
3. **Initiate repair attempts**— After conflicts, practice going back and saying: "I didn't handle that well. Can we try again?"
4. **Notice your patterns**— Do you consistently end up in relationships missing the same pillars? This may point to a schema or core belief to explore.
5. **Seek couples or relationship therapy**— when both people are willing. Progress is fastest with a skilled guide.

15

Guilt & Shame

Two Very Different Emotions

Guilt and shame are often used interchangeably, but they are fundamentally different emotional experiences with very different consequences for our mental health. Understanding this distinction is one of the most important things you can do for your healing journey.

Guilt: "I Did Something Bad"

- Focus is on the *behavior*
- Adaptive—tells us we violated our values
- Motivates repair and change
- There IS a path forward
- "I made a mistake" → I can fix it
- Leads to apology, amends, growth
- Appropriate guilt is healthy

Shame: "I AM Bad"

- Focus is on the *self*
- Maladaptive—attacks our core worth
- Motivates hiding, withdrawal, aggression
- There is NO clear path forward
- "I am a mistake" → unchangeable
- Leads to depression, rage, addiction
- Shame is almost never helpful

Example of the Difference

Guilt: "I lied to my friend about why I canceled. I feel terrible. I'm going to call them, tell the truth, and apologize."

Shame: "I lied to my friend. I'm such a terrible person. I'm the worst. I always ruin everything. I don't deserve good friends."

Brené Brown's Research on Shame

Researcher and author Brené Brown has spent over two decades studying shame and vulnerability. Her key findings include:

- Shame is **the most powerful master emotion**—the fear that we are fundamentally unworthy of love and belonging.
- Shame **thrives on secrecy, silence, and judgment**. Exposing it to the light—with empathy—is the primary antidote.
- The less we talk about shame, the **more control it has**

over us.

- Shame is highly correlated with addiction, depression, violence, aggression, and eating disorders.
- Guilt is inversely correlated with these outcomes—guilt actually *protects* us.

Brené Brown Quote

"Shame corrodes the very part of us that believes we are capable of change."—Brené Brown, *Daring Greatly*

Building Shame Resilience: The Three Components

1. Courage—Breaking the Silence

Shame requires secrecy to survive. The first act of resilience is daring to name what you are experiencing: "I'm feeling ashamed about this." You do not have to share it with everyone—but sharing it with *one* trusted person who has earned the right to hear it can be transformative. The story of "I'm unworthy" loses its power when spoken aloud and met with empathy instead of confirmation.

2. Empathy—The Antidote to Shame

Empathy does not fix, advise, or minimize. It says: *"I understand. I've been there too. You are not alone."* When we experience shame in the context of true empathy, the shame begins to dissolve. This is why therapy, support groups, and trusted friendships are healing. Connection—not isolation—is what breaks shame's hold.

3. Compassion—Replacing the Critical Voice

The final piece is turning toward yourself with the same warmth you would offer a close friend. Ask: "If my best friend told me they had done this same thing, what would I say to them?" Practice saying those same words to yourself. This is not about excusing harmful behavior—it is about separating your worth as a human being from your mistakes.

How to Monitor & Progress Through Guilt & Shame

1. **Identify guilt vs. shame**— When you feel bad about something, ask yourself: "Am I focusing on my behavior or on my worth as a person?" Use that distinction to choose your next step.
2. **Address guilt directly**— Make amends where possible and appropriate. Sitting in guilt without action keeps it chronic. Take one small step toward repair.
3. **Name shame in the moment**— Practice saying "I'm in a shame spiral right now" to yourself or a trusted person. Naming it reduces its power immediately.
4. **Track shame triggers**— What topics or situations consistently trigger your shame response? These often point directly to core schemas worth exploring in therapy.
5. **Write a compassion letter**— When shame strikes, write a letter to yourself from the perspective of a loving, wise mentor. What would they say about your worth as a person?

16

Self-Compassion

Self-compassion, developed and researched extensively by Dr. Kristin Neff, is the practice of treating yourself with the same kindness, concern, and understanding that you would offer a good friend who was struggling. It is not self-pity (which focuses inward and isolates), and it is not self-indulgence (giving yourself a pass on everything). It is honest, caring, and human.

Most of us have an inner critic—a harsh internal voice that judges us mercilessly when we fail, make mistakes, or fall short. This voice was often formed in childhood, echoing critical parents, teachers, or peers. Self-compassion is the practice of recognizing this voice, understanding its origins, and gradually replacing it with something more truthful and more kind.

The Question That Changes Everything

"How would you talk to a close friend going through exactly what you are going through right now?"—If your answer is different from how you talk to yourself, that gap is where self-compassion lives.

The Three Components of Self-Compassion (Dr. Kristin Neff)

1. Self-Kindness vs. Self-Judgment

Self-kindness means being warm and understanding toward ourselves when we suffer, fail, or feel inadequate, rather than ignoring our pain or flogging ourselves with self-criticism. It means acknowledging: "This is hard. I am struggling. I deserve care."

In Practice

Self-judgment: "I can't believe I said that. I'm such an idiot. Why do I always ruin things?"

Self-kindness: "That didn't come out the way I intended, and I feel embarrassed. It's okay to make mistakes. I'll try to clarify what I meant."

2. Common Humanity vs. Isolation

Suffering, failure, and feeling inadequate are *part of the shared human experience.* When we are in pain, we tend to feel isolated—like we are the only one who struggles this way, or that there must be something uniquely wrong with us. Common humanity recognizes: *Everyone fails. Everyone feels this. I am not alone in this.*

In Practice

Isolation: "Why can I never get it together? Everyone else seems fine."

Common humanity: "Millions of people feel this way.

Struggling does not make me abnormal—it makes me human."

3. Mindfulness vs. Over-Identification

Mindfulness in self-compassion means holding painful thoughts and feelings in balanced awareness—neither suppressing them nor exaggerating them. It is the ability to say: "I notice I'm feeling shame right now" rather than becoming entirely consumed by shame.

Self-Compassion vs. Self-Esteem

Self-esteem is contingent—it rises when we succeed and falls when we fail. It often depends on comparison with others, which means someone always has to lose. Self-compassion, by contrast, is *unconditional*. It does not require you to be better than others or even to feel good about yourself. It simply requires you to treat yourself as a decent human being who, like all human beings, is imperfect and worthy of care.

Research shows that self-compassion is associated with **greater emotional resilience, less anxiety and depression, more accurate self-perception, and healthier relationships**—without the downsides of narcissism or self-absorption that high self-esteem can produce.

The Inner Child Needs

Self-compassion is also about understanding what your inner child—the younger version of you who learned to cope with the world—needs from you *now*:

- The **Happy Child** needs: Encouragement, play, celebration
- The **Vulnerable Child** needs: Soothing, safety, gentle presence
- The **Angry Child** needs: Validation, acknowledgment of the injustice
- The **Impulsive Child** needs: Consistent, healthy limits (Fair, Firm, Forgive)

How to Monitor & Cultivate Self-Compassion

1. **Keep a self-compassion journal**— Each day, note one moment where you were self-critical, then rewrite it through a self-compassionate lens. Over weeks, notice how the reframe becomes more natural.
2. **Self-Compassion Break (Dr. Neff's practice)**— When struggling, say: "This is a moment of suffering. Suffering is part of life. May I be kind to myself in this moment."
3. **Notice the inner critic's language**— What words does it use? Whose voice does it sound like? Begin to separate that critical voice from your own identity.
4. **Body scan + kindness**— Where do you feel the self-criticism in your body? Place your hand there. Breathe. Offer that part of yourself warmth.
5. **Track the ratio**— For one week, note every self-critical comment you make internally, and practice one self-compassionate response for each. Notice if the ratio shifts.

17

Schemas

What Is a Schema?

A schema is a deeply embedded pattern or theme about yourself and your relationships with others. Think of it as a mental blueprint—a set of memories, emotions, body sensations, and beliefs that were formed early in life (usually childhood or adolescence) in response to unmet emotional needs or repeated painful experiences.

Schemas were originally developed by Dr. Jeffrey Young as an extension of Cognitive Behavioral Therapy. Where CBT focuses on surface-level automatic thoughts, Schema Therapy goes deeper—to the root system from which those thoughts grow. If negative thoughts are weeds, schemas are the root system underground that keeps producing them.

Key Insight

Schemas feel like absolute truths—but they are not facts. They are interpretations of experience formed when we were too young to know any better, and they are often wildly inaccurate when viewed through an adult lens.

How Schemas Form

Schemas develop when core childhood emotional needs go unmet. These needs include:

- **Safe attachment**—stability, security, consistent love
- **Autonomy & competence**—the ability to function independently
- **Freedom to express needs and emotions**
- **Spontaneity and play**
- **Realistic limits and self-control**

When these needs are consistently unmet—through neglect, abuse, over-control, loss, trauma, or criticism—schemas take root. They become the lens through which we filter all future experience.

Why Schemas Are So Persistent

Schemas persist for several reasons:

- **They feel familiar**—even painful schemas feel like "home." We gravitate toward people and situations that confirm what we already believe.
- **We avoid schema-triggering situations**—which prevents us from learning that our beliefs are false.
- **We misinterpret new evidence**—when something contradicts our schema, we often discount it or explain it away.
- **They are connected to emotion**—schemas are not just intellectual beliefs. They are tied to intense feelings,

which makes them feel much more real.

Example—The Abandonment Schema

Jamie grew up with a parent who was frequently absent due to illness. As an adult, Jamie has an Abandonment schema. When a romantic partner needs space or is unavailable, Jamie experiences intense panic and clingy behavior—even when the partner has given no reason for concern. The schema interprets neutral or minor events through the lens of "I will be left."

How to Monitor & Work Through Schemas

1. **Identify your schemas**— Complete the Young Schema Questionnaire (available with a therapist or online). Name the schemas that score highest.
2. **Track schema activation**— Keep a log of when you feel disproportionately upset. Ask: "Which schema might be driving this reaction?"
3. **Challenge with evidence**— Gather real evidence that contradicts your schema. Write it down. Read it when activated.
4. **Connect schema to origin**— With a therapist, explore where the schema came from. Understanding its origin reduces its authority.
5. **Practice "healthy adult" responses**— When a schema fires, practice responding as your Healthy Adult self would, rather than from the schema's automatic reaction.

18

Cognitive Behavioral Therapy

What Is CBT?

Cognitive Behavioral Therapy (CBT) is one of the most extensively researched and effective forms of psychotherapy available today. It is built on a fundamental insight: **it is not events themselves that disturb us, but the meaning we assign to them.** Our thoughts, feelings, and behaviors are intricately connected—change one, and you begin to change the others.

NAMI defines CBT as therapy that "focuses on exploring relationships among a person's thoughts, feelings, and behaviors. The core principles are identifying false beliefs and testing or challenging them." Studies have shown CBT to be effective for depression, anxiety, PTSD, OCD, eating disorders, substance use, and many other mental health challenges. Research further shows that CBT produces measurable changes in brain activity—it literally rewires how your brain processes information.

A Brief History

In the 1960s, psychiatrist Aaron T. Beck observed that his patients had a running internal dialogue—a stream of automatic thoughts—that profoundly affected their emotions and behavior. Beck called this approach "cognitive therapy." Over decades, behavioral techniques were integrated, creating the comprehensive framework now known as CBT. Today it is the most evidence-based form of psychological treatment in the world.

The ABC Model

The foundation of CBT is understanding the A-B-C connection:

- **A—Activating Event:** Something happens (objectively). "My boss didn't say hi to me in the hallway."
- **B—Beliefs & Thoughts:** How you interpret what happened. "She must be angry at me. I probably did something wrong. I might get fired."
- **C—Consequences:** The emotional and behavioral results of B. Anxiety, avoidance, inability to concentrate, snapping at family.

The key insight: **A does not cause C. B causes C.** The same event (A) can produce completely different consequences (C) depending on the interpretation (B). This means that by changing B, we can change C—without the external world changing at all.

The Cookie Story (CBT Illustration)

A woman at an airport buys cookies and sets them on the table while reading her paper. She watches in growing rage as a stranger helps himself to "her" cookies—until she opens her purse and discovers her own unopened package. She had been eating HIS cookies the whole time. Her feelings—real and intense as they were—were based on a completely incorrect interpretation of reality. This is CBT in a nutshell: feelings reflect what we believe, not necessarily what is true.

Automatic Thoughts & Cognitive Distortions

Automatic thoughts are knee-jerk mental responses—the first thing your mind offers when an event occurs. They happen so fast they often feel like facts rather than thoughts. When these thoughts are systematically distorted, they are called **cognitive distortions** (or ANTs—Automatic Negative Thoughts).

Common Cognitive Distortions

- **All-or-Nothing Thinking:** "If it's not perfect, it's a total failure." No grey area exists.
- **Catastrophizing:** "This headache must be a brain tumor." Expecting the worst possible outcome.
- **Mind Reading:** "I know they think I'm stupid"—without evidence.
- **Emotional Reasoning:** "I feel worthless, therefore I am worthless."
- **Overgeneralization:** "This always happens to me." One bad event = eternal pattern.
- **Personalization:** "They're in a bad mood—it must be

something I did."

- **Filtering:** Focusing only on the negatives while filtering out all the positives.
- **Should Statements:** Rigid rules about how you or others "must" behave that generate constant guilt or resentment.
- **Global Labeling:** "I failed that test → I am a failure" (as a human being).
- **Blaming:** Holding others entirely responsible for your pain, or yourself for everyone else's.

Identifying & Challenging a Distortion

Situation: Friend doesn't reply to your text for 6 hours.

Automatic Thought: "They're ignoring me. They must be angry. I did something wrong." (Mind Reading + Catastrophizing)

Challenge: "What is the evidence for this? What other explanations exist? They could be busy, in a meeting, asleep, dealing with something personal. Have I had a reason to reply slowly before? Yes. Is it possible they are not angry? Definitely."

Balanced Thought: "I don't know why they haven't replied yet. There are many possible explanations. I'll wait and see."

The Thought Record

A thought record is a core CBT tool used to slow down and examine automatic thoughts:

1. Describe the situation (just the facts)
2. Identify the emotion and rate its intensity (0–100%)
3. Identify the automatic thought
4. Identify which distortion(s) apply
5. Generate evidence FOR and AGAINST the thought
6. Write a more balanced, realistic alternative thought
7. Re-rate the emotion—it rarely goes to zero, but usually drops significantly

How to Monitor & Progress Through CBT Work

1. **Complete at least one thought record per week**targeting your most distressing recurring thought pattern. Notice how fluency builds over time.
2. **Track distortion frequency**— which distortions appear most in your records? This reveals your personal cognitive style and where to focus practice.
3. **Measure emotion intensity before and after**each thought record. Progress = decreasing intensity over time for similar triggers.
4. **Practice behavioral experiments**— Test your predictions in real life. "I believe my colleague dislikes me. Let me try saying good morning tomorrow and observe what actually happens."
5. **Notice delayed automatic thoughts**— As you improve, you'll catch thoughts later and later in the spiral. Eventually you'll catch them before they produce strong emotion.

19

Mindfulness

What Is Mindfulness?

Mindfulness is the practice of paying deliberate, non-judgmental attention to the present moment—to your thoughts, feelings, body sensations, and surrounding environment—exactly as they are, without trying to change, fix, or escape them.

It originates from ancient Buddhist meditation traditions and was brought into Western clinical psychology in the late 1970s by Jon Kabat-Zinn, who developed Mindfulness-Based Stress Reduction (MBSR). Today, mindfulness is one of the most empirically supported interventions in mental health, with hundreds of studies demonstrating its effectiveness for anxiety, depression, chronic pain, trauma, and everyday stress.

Key Principle

You cannot be mindful of the future (that is worry) or of the past (that is rumination). Mindfulness only exists in this moment, right now.

Why It Works—The Science

Research using brain imaging has shown that regular mindfulness practice:

- Reduces activity in the amygdala (the brain's alarm center)—meaning we react less intensely to stress
- Increases gray matter in the prefrontal cortex (reasoning and perspective-taking)
- Reduces the default mode network's "rumination loops"—the mental spinning that fuels depression and anxiety
- Increases awareness of body signals, which helps us catch emotion before it becomes overwhelming
- Reduces cortisol (the stress hormone) levels with regular practice

Core Mindfulness Skills

1. Observe

Watch your own thoughts, feelings, and sensations as if you are a curious scientist—without trying to change them. Imagine your thoughts as clouds passing across the sky. You are the sky, not the clouds. The clouds (thoughts) are not permanent, and they do not define you.

2. Describe

Put words to what you observe, without evaluation. Not "I'm having an anxiety attack" but "I notice my heart is beating quickly and my chest feels tight." Describing without judgment creates distance and reduces reactivity.

3. Participate

Fully engage in the present activity—not while scrolling, not while planning your response. Full immersion in what you are doing right now.

4. Non-Judgmentally

Observe without labeling things as "good" or "bad," "right" or "wrong." When you catch yourself judging—note "judging" and return to observing. This includes not judging your own judging.

5. One-Mindfully

Do one thing at a time. When eating, eat. When listening, listen. When walking, notice each step. Multitasking is the opposite of mindfulness.

Practical Exercises

5-4-3-2-1 Grounding

Name 5 things you can see, 4 you can touch, 3 you can hear, 2 you can smell, 1 you can taste. This anchors you in the present moment and is highly effective for anxiety and dissociation.

Box Breathing (4-4-4-4)

Inhale for 4 counts, hold for 4, exhale for 4, hold for 4. Repeat 4 times. This directly activates the parasympathetic nervous system, reducing stress within minutes.

Body Scan

Starting at the top of your head, slowly move your awareness down your body, noticing sensations—tension, warmth, tingling, heaviness—without trying to change them. This builds interoceptive awareness and reduces chronic tension.

RAIN Practice

- **R**ecognize—"I notice I'm feeling anxious."
- **A**llow—"It's okay that this is here right now."
- **I**nvestigate—"Where do I feel this in my body? What need is connected to this?"
- **N**ourish—"What does this part of me need right now?"

Example in Everyday Life

While washing dishes, instead of mentally rehearsing tomorrow's meeting, you focus on the warmth of the water, the smell of the soap, the sound of the water. Your mind wanders—you notice it, and gently return. This is a complete mindfulness practice. No meditation cushion required.

How to Monitor & Deepen Mindfulness Practice

1. **Start small:**5 minutes of formal practice daily is more effective than 60 minutes once a week. Use a timer. No phone.
2. **Use an app**(Headspace, Calm, Insight Timer) for guided practice, especially in the early stages. Track your streak.
3. **Notice the gap**— between stimulus and response—growing wider over time. This gap is mindfulness. When you respond rather than react, you are progressing.
4. **Weekly reflection**— At the end of each week, ask: "How present was I this week? What pulled me most into the past or future?"
5. **Bring mindfulness into daily activities:**eating one meal mindfully, taking one shower paying full attention. Progress is not just formal practice—it is moment-to-moment awareness in life.

20

Adequacy

Reframing What "Enough" Means

Culture tells us that "adequate" is a failure—a consolation prize for those who didn't try hard enough. Words like "average," "sufficient," and "good enough" carry shame in a society obsessed with optimization, metrics, and achievement. We have been conditioned to believe that anything short of exceptional is unworthy of pride.

But this cultural definition is doing tremendous harm. It feeds perfectionism, burnout, chronic self-doubt, and an inability to enjoy our own accomplishments. A healthier, more accurate definition of adequacy is: **meeting the genuine needs of a situation with the resources available to you at the time.**

Culture's Definition

- Barely good enough
- Not perfect = failure
- Just okay / mediocre

- Average = shameful
- Mid / settling

Reality's Definition

- Genuinely good enough
- Competent and capable
- Suitable for the situation
- Satisfactory given circumstances
- Worthy of self-respect

Whose Expectations Are We Meeting?

Before judging whether you've been "adequate," ask: adequate by whose standard? Often we are measuring ourselves against standards we never consciously chose—absorbed from critical parents, competitive schools, social media highlight reels, or cultural pressures. The question "Did I do my best, given the actual circumstances of this specific day?" is a far more honest and useful measuring stick.

Perfectionism: The Dark Side of High Standards

Perfectionism is often mistaken for having high standards. In reality, it is a defense mechanism rooted in fear. The perfectionist sets impossible standards not because they love excellence—but because they fear that without perfect performance, they are unworthy of love, acceptance, or safety. Key markers of perfectionism include:

- Motivation driven by fear of failure rather than genuine

enthusiasm

- Feeling that no accomplishment—however significant—is ever truly satisfying
- Believing you must earn love, affection, or respect through performance
- All-or-nothing thinking: "If it's not perfect, it's worthless"
- Extreme distress when outcomes don't match expectations
- Continuing to pursue impossible standards despite significant personal cost

The Adequacy Mindset (Historian Rachel Judith Weil)

"Let's drop the exhortations to fail or suck at something and instead cultivate the adequacy mindset—the feeling of being proud and grateful to be good enough to continue doing something from which we get pleasure and knowledge."

A More Honest Measure of Success

Ask yourself these two questions instead of comparing your output to an impossible ideal:

1. **"Did I do the best I could, given the actual circumstances today?"**
2. **"Even if I don't love the outcome, is there something I can learn from this?"**

Note: "given the circumstances" is doing a lot of work here. A single parent who worked all day and still managed to cook dinner for their kids has done something remarkable—even if the meal was simple. Context matters enormously.

Example

Alex turns in a project that is solid, thorough, and on time—but not what they imagined it could have been with two more weeks of work. The perfectionist voice says "This isn't good enough." The adequacy mindset says: "Given my timeline, my other responsibilities, and my energy this week, I did my best and this work is genuinely good. I can improve next time."

How to Monitor & Cultivate Adequacy

1. **Daily adequacy check**— At day's end, ask: "Given today's actual circumstances (sleep, stress, demands), did I do what was reasonable?" Rate 1–10 based on *effort in context*, not on outcomes.
2. **Track perfectionism triggers**— Notice which areas of life activate perfectionism most (work, parenting, appearance, relationships). These often link to core schemas.
3. **Practice "good enough" deliberately**— Choose one low-stakes task each week and intentionally do it to "good enough" standard rather than perfection. Notice what happens.
4. **Challenge the standard**— When you feel inadequate, ask: "Is this standard realistic? Would I hold a friend to this standard? Where did this standard come from?"
5. **Celebrate adequacy**— Actively acknowledge and feel proud of things you did adequately. They deserve recognition too.

21

Schema Modes

What Are Schema Modes?

Schema modes are the different emotional states and coping responses that we "flip" between in daily life. While schemas are deep, stable patterns, **modes are the moment-to-moment expression of those schemas**—the current emotional state you are in right now, being driven by a schema that has been activated.

Think of modes as different internal "parts" or "characters" within you. A person might shift from the Vulnerable Child mode (feeling small and scared) to the Punitive Parent mode (attacking themselves) to the Detached Protector mode (numbing out) all within a single difficult conversation. The goal of Schema Therapy is to strengthen the **Healthy Adult** mode—the part of you that can observe these shifts, care for the child parts, set limits on the critic parts, and choose wise responses.

The Four Categories of Schema Modes

Category 1: Child Modes

These represent the emotional experiences of our younger selves:

- **Vulnerable Child:** Feels sad, lonely, unloved, afraid, ashamed, or worthless. This is the core wound—the part that is hurting most deeply. Needs: soothing, safety, compassion.
- **Angry Child:** Feels rage at perceived injustice or unmet needs. The anger is legitimate but may be expressed inappropriately. Needs: validation that the anger makes sense, appropriate expression channels.
- **Impulsive/Undisciplined Child:** Acts on immediate desires without considering consequences. Lives for instant gratification. Needs: fair, firm, consistent limits.
- **Happy/Contented Child:** Feels safe, loved, playful, and curious. This is what we are working toward—a part that has experienced enough safety to simply be.

Category 2: Dysfunctional Parent Modes

These are internalized voices of critical or demanding caregivers:

- **Punitive Parent:** Attacks, criticizes, and punishes the self. "You are worthless." "You deserved that." "You should be ashamed." This mode generates overwhelming shame and self-hatred. It needs to be banished—not negotiated with.

- **Demanding Parent:** Pushes for impossible standards, relentless achievement, perfect compliance. "You must be better. You're not doing enough. You haven't earned rest." This mode generates exhaustion, anxiety, and burnout.

Identifying a Parent Mode

After making a small mistake, Jordan immediately hears: "You are such an idiot. You always screw this up. What is wrong with you?"—This is the Punitive Parent mode speaking. It sounds factual, but it is a harmful internal voice, not objective truth.

Category 3: Coping Modes

These developed in childhood to protect us from pain—but in adulthood, they prevent healing:

- **Detached Protector:** Emotional numbness, detachment, withdrawal. "I don't feel anything." "Nothing matters." Cuts off from both pain and connection.
- **Compliant Surrenderer:** Submits to others to avoid conflict or abandonment. Goes along with everything, even at the cost of their own needs. People-pleasing.
- **Overcompensator:** Fights back against the schema by going to the opposite extreme. E.g., someone with a Defectiveness schema becomes arrogant and dismissive of others to avoid feeling inadequate.
- **Bully/Attack:** Aggression, intimidation, or control of others to avoid feeling vulnerable.
- **Self-Aggrandizer:** Seeks constant admiration and supe-

riority to compensate for deep feelings of worthlessness.

Category 4: The Healthy Adult Mode

This is the goal—the wise, compassionate, functional part of you. The Healthy Adult:

- Nurtures and soothes the Vulnerable Child
- Validates and appropriately expresses the Angry Child
- Sets fair, consistent limits for the Impulsive Child
- Challenges and dismisses the Punitive Parent
- Moderates the Demanding Parent with realistic standards
- Gradually replaces coping modes with authentic engagement

How to Monitor & Strengthen Healthy Adult Mode

1. **Mode mapping**— Draw a diagram of your most common modes. When do each appear? What triggers them? What do they say or do?
2. **Catch mode shifts in real time**— Practice asking: "Which mode am I in right now?" even once per day. Awareness precedes change.
3. **Practice mode dialogue**— In journaling or with a therapist, let your Healthy Adult "speak to" the Vulnerable Child or challenge the Punitive Parent. What would a truly good parent say?
4. **Build the Healthy Adult intentionally**— List 5 qualities you want in your HA: wise, compassionate, firm, patient, curious. Practice embodying one quality per week.

5. **Notice coping mode costs**— Each time you detach, comply, or overcompensate, briefly note: "What need was I avoiding? What did this cost me?"

22

Early Maladaptive Schemas (EMS)

What Are Early Maladaptive Schemas?

Early Maladaptive Schemas (EMS) are broad, pervasive themes or patterns about oneself and one's relationship with others that developed during childhood and adolescence, were dysfunctional to a significant degree, and were reinforced throughout life. There are **18 identified schemas** organized into 5 domains. Each schema is a package of memories, emotions, bodily sensations, and beliefs about oneself and the world.

The word "maladaptive" is key: these schemas were *adaptive when they first formed.* A child who is repeatedly abandoned learns to expect abandonment—and this expectation is protective. The problem is that these patterns don't update when circumstances change in adulthood. They keep running, applying an outdated map to new territory.

The 18 Early Maladaptive Schemas

Domain 1: Disconnection & Rejection

- **Abandonment/Instability:** The belief that significant others will not continue to provide support, connection, strength, or protection because they are emotionally unstable, or are unreliable—or will abandon you for someone better. *Core fear: Everyone leaves eventually.*
- **Mistrust/Abuse:** The expectation that others will hurt, abuse, humiliate, cheat, lie, manipulate, or take advantage of you. *Core fear: People cannot be trusted.*
- **Emotional Deprivation:** The expectation that one's desire for emotional support—nurturance, empathy, protection, guidance—will not be adequately met by others. *Core fear: My needs will never be met.*
- **Defectiveness/Shame:** The feeling that one is defective, bad, unwanted, inferior, or unlovable in important respects; or that one would be fundamentally unlovable to significant others if exposed. *Core fear: If people really knew me, they would reject me.*
- **Social Isolation/Alienation:** The feeling that one is isolated from the rest of the world, different from other people, and not part of any group or community. *Core fear: I don't belong anywhere.*

Domain 2: Impaired Autonomy & Performance

- **Dependence/Incompetence:** Belief that one is unable to handle everyday responsibilities competently without considerable help from others. *Core fear: I cannot function on my own.*
- **Vulnerability to Harm or Illness:** Exaggerated fear that

imminent catastrophe (medical, emotional, natural) will strike at any time and one will be unable to cope. *Core fear: Something terrible is about to happen.*

- **Enmeshment/Undeveloped Self:** Excessive emotional involvement and closeness with one or more significant others, at the expense of full individuation or normal social development. *Core fear: I don't know who I am without them.*
- **Failure:** The belief that one has failed, will inevitably fail, or is fundamentally inadequate relative to one's peers in areas of achievement. *Core fear: I am a born failure.*

Domain 3: Impaired Limits

- **Entitlement/Grandiosity:** The belief that one is superior to other people—entitled to special rights and privileges, or not bound by rules of reciprocity. *Core fear: I must be in control and on top to be safe.*
- **Insufficient Self-Control/Self-Discipline:** Pervasive difficulty or refusal to exercise sufficient self-control and frustration tolerance to achieve personal goals. *Core fear: I cannot tolerate discomfort.*

Domain 4: Other-Directedness

- **Subjugation:** Excessive surrendering of control to others because one feels coerced—usually to avoid anger, retaliation, or abandonment. *Core fear: My needs and feelings don't matter.*
- **Self-Sacrifice:** Excessive focus on voluntarily meeting the needs of others at the expense of one's own gratifica-

tion. *Core fear: If I take care of myself, I am selfish.*

- **Approval-Seeking/Recognition-Seeking:** Excessive emphasis on gaining approval, recognition, or attention from other people. *Core fear: I must be validated to have worth.*

Domain 5: Overvigilance & Inhibition

- **Negativity/Pessimism:** A pervasive, lifelong focus on the negative aspects of life while minimizing the positive. *Core fear: Something will always go wrong.*
- **Emotional Inhibition:** The excessive inhibition of spontaneous action, feeling, or communication—usually to avoid disapproval, shame, or loss of control. *Core fear: Showing emotions is dangerous or wrong.*
- **Unrelenting Standards/Hypercriticalness:** The belief that one must strive to meet very high internalized standards, usually to avoid criticism. *Core fear: If I'm not perfect, I am worthless.*
- **Punitiveness:** The belief that people (including oneself) should be harshly punished for making mistakes. *Core fear: Mistakes deserve punishment, not understanding.*

How to Monitor & Heal EMS

1. **Complete the YSQ**— Young Schema Questionnaire (short form available online). Identify your top 3–5 schemas. Focus there first.
2. **Trace the schema to its origin**— With a therapist, identify the early experiences that gave rise to each schema. Understanding the origin helps depersonalize

the schema.

3. **Compile a "schema diary"**— For 2 weeks, note each time a strong emotion arises and which schema might be driving it. Patterns will emerge.
4. **Challenge schema beliefs with evidence**— Especially gather evidence that contradicts the schema. Schema evidence logs are powerful homework tools.
5. **Imagery rescripting**— With a therapist, revisit a formative schema memory and rewrite it with the protection and nurturing the younger you needed. This is one of the most powerful interventions.

23

Schema Avoidance (EAs / Coping Styles)

What Are Schema Coping Styles?

When a schema is activated—when something triggers that deep, painful core belief—the mind and body launch a protective response. These protective responses are called **schema coping styles** (also called Emotional Avoidance strategies or EAs). They were developed to protect us from the overwhelming pain of schema activation. The problem: while they reduce pain in the short term, they perpetuate and strengthen the schema over time.

There are three primary coping styles, often remembered as **surrender, avoidance, and overcompensation**. Most people have a preferred coping style, though we may use all three in different situations.

The Paradox

The very strategies we use to protect ourselves from schema pain are the strategies that keep the schema alive. Healing requires gradually reducing reliance on coping behaviors—which at first feels very threatening.

The Three Schema Coping Styles

1. Schema Surrender

The person gives in to the schema—acts as if it is completely true—and behaves in ways that confirm it. They repeat patterns that recreate the original painful dynamic.

Example

Alex has an Abandonment schema. Rather than challenging this belief, Alex clings desperately to partners, demands constant reassurance, and becomes highly controlling—behaviors that eventually drive partners away, confirming: "See? Everyone leaves me." The schema is surrendered to and reinforced.

2. Schema Avoidance

The person avoids people, places, feelings, or situations that might trigger the schema. On the surface, they may seem fine—but they are operating in a severely restricted world, missing out on meaningful experiences to avoid pain.

- **Cognitive avoidance:** Refusing to think about painful topics, blocking memories
- **Emotional avoidance:** Numbing, dissociation, substance use, excessive TV/social media
- **Behavioral avoidance:** Not applying for jobs (Failure schema), not entering relationships (Abandonment schema), not seeking help (Subjugation schema)

Example

Sam has a Defectiveness schema. To avoid ever being "seen"

and found inadequate, Sam avoids social gatherings, never shares personal opinions, and keeps relationships superficial. The schema is never challenged because Sam never receives contradicting evidence (genuine acceptance).

3. Schema Overcompensation

The person fights against the schema by going to the opposite extreme—overcorrecting so aggressively that they create new problems. This can look like success on the outside, while hiding intense pain underneath.

Example

Chris has a Defectiveness/Shame schema but presents as arrogant, dismissive, and superior to others. The overcompensation protects against the underlying feeling of being worthless, but drives people away and prevents authentic connection.

Common Specific Avoidance Strategies

- Alcohol and drug use to numb schema pain
- Workaholism (avoiding intimacy or failure schema triggers)
- Over-eating or restrictive eating
- Compulsive sex or avoidance of sex
- Excessive exercise as self-punishment or control
- Chronic busy-ness (never sitting still with one's own thoughts)
- Excessive caretaking of others (avoids focusing on own needs)
- Intellectualizing everything (avoids feeling)

How to Monitor & Reduce Schema Avoidance

1. **Identify your preferred coping style**— For each of your top schemas, ask: Do I tend to surrender (repeat the pattern), avoid (restrict my life), or overcompensate (do the opposite extreme)?
2. **Map avoidance behaviors**— List the specific behaviors you use to avoid schema pain. Be honest. These are the behaviors to gradually reduce.
3. **Gradual exposure**— With therapeutic support, begin approaching schema-triggering situations in small, manageable steps rather than completely avoiding them. Avoidance maintains anxiety; exposure reduces it.
4. **Track the short-term relief vs. long-term cost**— After using a coping behavior, note: "This felt better for ___ hours, but the long-term cost is ___."
5. **Develop healthy alternatives**— For each avoidance behavior, identify a healthier way to meet the same underlying need. (e.g., instead of numbing with alcohol, call a trusted friend).

24

Core Beliefs

The Deepest Layer of Thought

In the cognitive model of psychotherapy, our thinking operates at three levels: automatic thoughts (surface), intermediate beliefs (middle), and core beliefs (deepest). Core beliefs are the absolute, global, rigid beliefs about yourself, others, and the world that form the foundation of your entire way of seeing reality. They function like operating system code—running constantly in the background, shaping every thought and interpretation above them.

Core beliefs are not usually consciously chosen. They are formed through repeated experience—especially in early life—and they feel so natural and obvious that we rarely question them. They feel less like "beliefs" and more like facts.

Key Insight

Core beliefs feel like facts: "I am worthless." But they are interpretations—formed by a young mind responding to painful experiences. They are not objective truth about who you are.

Three Categories of Core Beliefs

1. Core Beliefs About Self

- "I am worthless." / "I am unlovable."
- "I am stupid." / "I am a failure."
- "I am bad." / "I am broken."
- "I am a burden." / "I am unwanted."
- "I can't trust myself." / "I am incompetent."

2. Core Beliefs About Others

- "People will hurt me." / "No one can be trusted."
- "People will leave me." / "No one really cares."
- "People only want things from me." / "Everyone is out for themselves."
- "Others are more capable than me." / "I will always be judged."

3. Core Beliefs About the World/Future

- "The world is dangerous." / "Life is unfair."
- "Good things don't last." / "Bad things always happen to me."
- "There is no point trying." / "Things will never change."

How Core Beliefs Operate: The Self-Fulfilling Prophecy

Core beliefs do not stay quietly in the background. They actively shape what we notice, how we interpret it, and what we do in response—creating a self-reinforcing loop:

1. Core belief: "I am unlovable."
2. Filter: Notice every rejection, discount every expression of care.
3. Behavior: Avoid closeness, push people away before they can reject you.
4. Outcome: Relationships are superficial or end. "See? I was right."

Example in Daily Life

Jordan holds the core belief "I am a failure." When Jordan does well on a project, the automatic thought is: "That was just luck—anyone could have done that." When Jordan makes a mistake: "This proves it. I'm hopeless." The core belief filters every piece of evidence to maintain itself.

Intermediate Beliefs: The Bridge Layer

Between core beliefs and automatic thoughts sit **intermediate beliefs**—rules, assumptions, and attitudes that translate core beliefs into behavioral guidelines. They typically take forms like:

- "If _____, then _____." (Conditional assumptions)
- "I must _______ or else _______." (Rules)
- "People who ________ are _________." (Attitudes)

Example: Core belief "I am unlovable" → Intermediate belief "If I don't make everyone happy, they will leave me" → Automatic thought "She looked disappointed. I need to fix this immediately or she'll leave."

How to Monitor & Shift Core Beliefs

1. **Identify your core beliefs**— Use the downward arrow technique with a therapist: "If that were true, what would that mean about you?" Keep going until you reach the absolute bottom.
2. **Rate belief strength**— On a scale of 0–100%, how strongly do you believe this core belief right now? Track this weekly. Progress = gradually decreasing strength.
3. **Keep a positive data log**— Actively collect evidence that contradicts the core belief daily. Because the belief filters out contradicting evidence, you must deliberately look for it.
4. **Historical review**— With a therapist, examine the origin of the core belief. What experiences created it? Could a child have interpreted those experiences differently? Was the child's conclusion accurate?
5. **Behavioral experiments**— Test the core belief directly. If you believe "I am unlovable," practice vulnerability with one trusted person and observe what actually happens.

25

5 Schema Domains

Understanding the Domains

Dr. Jeffrey Young organized the 18 Early Maladaptive Schemas into **5 broad domains**, each representing a cluster of related unmet childhood needs. Each domain reflects a particular way that early relationships and experiences failed to provide what a developing child needed. Understanding which domain is most active for you helps focus therapy.

Domain 1: Disconnection & Rejection

Core theme: The belief that one's needs for safety, security, stability, nurturance, empathy, sharing of feelings, acceptance, and belonging will not be met in a predictable manner.

Typical family origin: Families that are cold, rejecting, withholding, abusive, explosive, unpredictable, or neglectful.

Schemas in this domain:

- **Abandonment/Instability:** Fear that even loved ones will leave. Hypervigilance to signs of rejection. Clinginess or preemptive distancing.
- **Mistrust/Abuse:** Expectation of being hurt, abused, or manipulated. Difficulty trusting anyone. May stay in abusive relationships (familiar) or avoid all intimacy.
- **Emotional Deprivation:** Persistent feeling that emotional needs (for nurturance, empathy, protection) will never be met. Chooses unavailable partners. Difficulty asking for help.
- **Defectiveness/Shame:** Core feeling of being fundamentally flawed, bad, unworthy. Extreme sensitivity to criticism. Hiding "the real self."
- **Social Isolation/Alienation:** Feeling different from everyone else, not belonging anywhere. Difficulty feeling genuinely part of any group.

Example—Domain 1

Maya grew up with a highly critical, emotionally distant father. She developed both a Defectiveness schema ("there is something wrong with me") and an Emotional Deprivation schema ("no one will ever really be there for me"). In adulthood, she attracts emotionally unavailable partners—confirming both schemas simultaneously.

Domain 2: Impaired Autonomy & Performance

Core theme: Beliefs about oneself and the environment that interfere with one's perceived ability to separate, survive, function independently, or perform successfully.

Typical family origin: Overprotective families that do not allow the child to develop independent competence, or chaotic families where the child never felt safe or capable.

Schemas in this domain:

- **Dependence/Incompetence:** "I can't handle life without help." Difficulty making decisions. Constant reassurance-seeking. Feeling like an adult playing dress-up.
- **Vulnerability to Harm:** Living in a constant state of low-grade catastrophizing. Health anxiety, fear of disaster, hypochondria. Chronic hypervigilance.
- **Enmeshment/Undeveloped Self:** Unclear personal identity, fused with a parent or partner. "I don't know what I think/feel/want without referencing another person."
- **Failure:** "I am fundamentally incompetent compared to others." Underachievement, avoidance of challenges, convinced success is luck and failure is inevitable.

Domain 3: Impaired Limits

Core theme: Deficiency in internal limits, responsibility to others, or long-term goal orientation. Difficulty respecting the rights of others or meeting personal commitments.

Typical family origin: Permissive or indulgent families that did not set appropriate limits, teach responsibility, or model frustration tolerance.

Schemas in this domain:

- **Entitlement/Grandiosity:** "Rules don't apply to me." Difficulty with reciprocity, empathy, and accepting limits. May present as narcissism—but often covers deep shame.
- **Insufficient Self-Control:** Chronic impulsivity, difficulty completing tasks, low frustration tolerance. Acts on immediate impulse despite long-term consequences.

Domain 4: Other-Directedness

Core theme: An excessive focus on the desires, feelings, and responses of others, at the expense of one's own needs, in order to gain love or approval, avoid retaliation, or maintain connection.

Typical family origin: Families in which love was conditional on meeting parents' needs; or family with a very dominant, critical, or needy parent.

Schemas in this domain:

- **Subjugation:** Systematic suppression of own needs and feelings to avoid others' anger or retaliation. "My feelings/needs don't matter." Chronic resentment underneath compliance.
- **Self-Sacrifice:** Voluntarily meeting others' needs at one's own expense. Feels guilty resting or receiving. Attracts

needy partners. Burnout is common.

- **Approval-Seeking:** Self-worth entirely contingent on external validation. Chameleon-like—changes personality to suit different audiences. Difficulty knowing authentic preferences.

Domain 5: Overvigilance & Inhibition

Core theme: Excessive emphasis on suppressing feelings, impulses, and choices, or on following rigid internal rules and expectations about performance and ethical behavior—often at the expense of happiness, self-expression, relaxation, and health.

Typical family origin: Families with very high standards, strict rules, punishment-focused discipline, or significant pessimism and anxiety about the world.

Schemas in this domain:

- **Negativity/Pessimism:** Pervasive focus on what could go wrong. Difficulty enjoying positive events. Chronic worry and expecting the worst.
- **Emotional Inhibition:** Suppression of emotions, spontaneity, or play—for fear of disapproval or loss of control. "Emotions are weak/dangerous/wrong."
- **Unrelenting Standards:** Perfectionism driven by fear. Must always achieve more, do better. Rest = laziness = shame. Driven but never satisfied.
- **Punitiveness:** Belief that mistakes deserve harsh punishment. Extremely self-critical. Difficulty forgiving self or others. May be attracted to punishing relationships.

How to Work Through the 5 Domains

1. **Identify your primary domain**— Which cluster of schemas feels most like your lived experience? Start there.
2. **Connect to unmet childhood needs**— What did you need as a child that you didn't receive? Name it specifically. This is the need your Healthy Adult can now begin to meet.
3. **Schema diary by domain**— For two weeks, keep notes organized by domain. Which domain is most active in your daily emotional life?
4. **Flashcard work**— Write one card per schema: "I know I have this schema. But the healthy truth is ___." Read daily, especially when activated.
5. **Targeted therapy**— Work with a schema-trained therapist to address the domain with the most disruption through imagery rescripting and mode work.

26

Good Parent Letter

What Is a Good Parent Letter?

A Good Parent Letter is a therapeutic writing exercise used in Schema Therapy to provide the healing experience of being nurtured, protected, and validated—the experience that was missing or insufficient in childhood. It is a letter written from the perspective of the "ideal parent" you needed but may not have fully had: a parent who is unconditionally loving, safe, wise, consistent, and attuned to your needs.

The purpose is not to blame real parents—most parents did their best within their own limitations and histories. The purpose is to give your inner child the messages they needed to hear, which the adult you can now provide through this practice of **reparenting.**

The Core Principle

We cannot change the past. But we can change our relationship to the past, and we can give ourselves—in the present—the nurturing that was missing then. This is what reparenting is.

The Four Child Needs Addressed in Good Parent Letters

- **Soothing**—For the Vulnerable Child who is scared, sad, or lonely. The letter brings warmth, safety, and calm.
- **Encouragement**—For the Happy/Striving Child. The letter celebrates genuine effort and supports exploration.
- **Validation**—For the Angry Child whose anger at injustice makes sense. The letter acknowledges: "Your anger is understandable and legitimate."
- **Consistent, Fair Limits**—For the Impulsive Child who needs structure without punishment. The letter is firm and caring: "I understand you want this. Here is what is safe and what is not."

How to Write a Good Parent Letter

The letter is written in second person (to your younger self) from the perspective of the ideal parent:

1. **Choose a specific situation:** A current or past situation where your inner child part is activated—fear, shame, loneliness, impulsivity, etc.
2. **Identify the need:** Which child mode is present? What does that part need right now?
3. **Write as the Good Parent:** Speak directly to the child. Use "I" (the parent) and "you" (the child). Be warm, specific, and concrete.
4. **Include:** Acknowledgment of the feeling, unconditional love/acceptance, protection, guidance, and encouragement.
5. **Read it aloud**—slowly, to yourself. Let it land. It may

feel awkward or produce emotion. Both are normal and good signs.

Example Good Parent Letter

Example Letter—Addressing the Vulnerable Child

"Dear little one,

I see you hiding. I know you are afraid that if you speak up, something bad will happen—that you'll be laughed at, dismissed, or left. That fear makes complete sense. You learned early on that it wasn't safe to be seen.

But I need you to know something: you are not alone anymore. I am here, and I am not going anywhere. You do not have to earn my love or my presence. You have it—fully, unconditionally—simply because you exist.

It is okay to need things. It is okay to feel scared. I will not punish you for your feelings. I will not leave when things get hard. I am here, and I am strong enough to hold this with you.

You deserve to be loved exactly as you are. Not a fixed version. Not a quieter version. You—exactly as you are—right now.

I love you. I've got you. All my love, [Your Healthy Adult Self]"

How to Monitor Progress with Good Parent Letters

1. **Write one letter per week**initially, targeting your most frequently activated child mode. Notice whether the words feel increasingly natural over time.
2. **Rate your emotional response**– Before and after each letter, rate how distressed the child mode feels (0–10). Progress = decreasing distress and increasing capacity to be soothed by your own words.
3. **Keep a letter journal**– Collect your letters over months. Reading earlier letters can show you how far you've come and which themes keep appearing.
4. **Notice real-world changes**– Are you treating yourself more gently after conflict? Are you quicker to self-soothe? These are signs the inner parent is strengthening.
5. **Share with your therapist**– Good Parent Letters are most powerful when processed with a therapist who can reflect and deepen the work.

27

Emotions 101

What Are Emotions?

Emotions are complex psychophysiological experiences—involving the body, the mind, and behavior—that arise in response to internal or external stimuli. They are not weaknesses, character flaws, or irrationalities. Emotions are **information**. They evolved over millions of years to help us navigate our world, connect with others, and survive. Every emotion serves a function.

Psychologist Robert Plutchik identified **8 primary emotions** from which all other emotions are derived, much like primary colors from which all others are mixed. These are: **Joy, Sadness, Trust, Disgust, Fear, Anger, Surprise, and Anticipation.**

Plutchik's Wheel of Emotions

Plutchik arranged emotions in a "wheel" to show their relationships and intensities:

- **Joy** (low intensity: Serenity → high intensity: Ecstasy)—Tells us: this is good, pursue this
- **Sadness** (Pensiveness → Grief)—Tells us: we have experienced a loss; signals others to provide care
- **Trust** (Acceptance → Admiration)—Tells us: this is safe and good for connection
- **Disgust** (Boredom → Loathing)—Tells us: this is harmful or wrong; reject/distance
- **Fear** (Apprehension → Terror)—Tells us: danger is present; mobilize for protection
- **Anger** (Annoyance → Rage)—Tells us: a boundary has been violated; act to protect
- **Surprise** (Distraction → Amazement)—Tells us: something unexpected has occurred; pay attention
- **Anticipation** (Interest → Vigilance)—Tells us: something is coming; prepare

The Function of Emotions

Every emotion has a purpose. The goal is not to eliminate uncomfortable emotions but to **understand what they are communicating and respond wisely:**

Emotion → Message → Action

- **Anxiety:** "Something needs attention" → Assess & prepare
- **Anger:** "A boundary was crossed" → Communicate or protect
- **Sadness:** "I experienced a loss" → Grieve, connect, receive support

- **Guilt:** "I acted outside my values" → Make amends, change behavior
- **Fear:** "There is danger" → Assess & respond appropriately
- **Shame:** "I feel unworthy" → Challenge the belief, seek connection

What Happens When We Suppress

- Emotions don't disappear—they go underground
- Suppressed emotions intensify over time
- They emerge sideways (anger as sarcasm, sadness as numbness)
- They manifest physically (tension, headaches, illness)
- They drive impulsive behavior
- "What you resist, persists"—Carl Jung

Building Emotional Literacy

Many people were never taught to identify, name, or express emotions—especially if their family system punished or dismissed emotional expression. Emotional literacy is the ability to recognize and name emotions precisely. Research by Lisa Feldman Barrett shows that the more precisely you can name an emotion (*granularity*), the better you can regulate it.

Instead of "I feel bad," try: "I feel ashamed, lonely, and helpless." The specificity allows for a targeted response.

The RULER Approach (Yale Center for Emotional Intelligence)

- **Recognize**—Notice an emotion is present in yourself or others
- **Understand**—Know what caused the emotion
- **Label**—Name it accurately and specifically
- **Express**—Share it appropriately, given the context
- **Regulate**—Manage the emotional experience effectively

Building Emotional Vocabulary

Instead of: "I'm angry" → Try: "I'm feeling humiliated and powerless"

Instead of: "I'm sad" → Try: "I'm feeling lonely, nostalgic, and a little hopeless"

Instead of: "I'm fine" → Try: pausing and genuinely checking in with yourself first

How to Monitor & Improve Emotional Intelligence

1. **Daily emotion check-in**— Set an alarm 3x/day. When it goes off, pause and name what you're feeling specifically. Track in a journal or app.
2. **Expand your vocabulary**— Download a feelings wheel. When you notice an emotion, find the most precise word on the wheel. Practice weekly.
3. **Track the body first**— Emotions live in the body before the mind processes them. Where in your body do you feel anxiety? Sadness? Anger? Build an emotion-body map for yourself.
4. **Practice the pause**— Before responding to a strong

emotion, name it: "I notice I am feeling ____." The naming itself reduces intensity.

5. **Review weekly**— Which emotions appeared most this week? Are there any you consistently avoid feeling? What might they be communicating?

28

Occupational Therapy Education

What Is Occupational Therapy?

Occupational Therapy (OT) is a health profession focused on helping people engage meaningfully in the activities ("occupations") that give their lives meaning and structure—including self-care, work, leisure, education, social participation, and rest. Unlike popular belief, OT is not just for physical rehabilitation. It is deeply intertwined with mental health and is one of the most comprehensive wellness approaches available.

The word "occupation" in OT does not mean a job. It means *any meaningful activity that occupies your time and gives life purpose.* This includes cooking, parenting, hobbies, friendships, creative pursuits, spiritual practices, and daily routines.

Core OT Principle

Meaningful activity is therapeutic. When we engage in purposeful occupations that match our values, abilities, and environment, mental health improves. When we lose access to meaningful occupation, mental health deteriorates.

OT's Role in Mental Health

Mental health OT addresses the **functional impact** of mental health challenges—the ways that depression, anxiety, trauma, or psychosis affect a person's ability to live their daily life. OT practitioners work to:

- Assess what a person can and cannot do in their daily life, and why
- Identify which occupations bring meaning and which create distress
- Build skills for managing daily tasks during mental health challenges
- Design personalized routines that support stability and recovery
- Teach coping strategies embedded in real-world activities
- Address the physical manifestations of mental health (sleep, self-care, exercise)

The 5 Areas of Occupation

1. Activities of Daily Living (ADLs)

Basic self-care: bathing, dressing, grooming, eating, toileting. When depression or anxiety makes these feel impossible, OT helps break them into achievable steps and rebuild them as sustainable routines.

2. Instrumental ADLs

Higher-level daily activities: managing finances, cooking, driving, using technology, caring for others, medication management. Mental health challenges can disrupt any of these significantly.

3. Work & Productive Occupation

Employment, volunteering, education. OT supports people in maintaining, returning to, or finding new forms of productive engagement—including building workplace coping strategies and managing symptoms in professional environments.

4. Leisure & Rest

The ability to rest without guilt and engage in enjoyable activities is a core component of mental wellness. OT helps people identify meaningful leisure activities and build the capacity to actually rest—which is harder than it sounds for many people with anxiety, hypervigilance, or schema-driven workaholism.

5. Social Participation

Relationships with family, friends, and community. OT addresses the social barriers created by mental health challenges—helping people rebuild and maintain social connections.

Key OT Concepts for Mental Health

Routine & Structure

Predictable routines reduce anxiety, support medication adherence, regulate sleep, and create a scaffold for recovery. OT helps you design a daily and weekly routine that is both realistic and recovery-supporting.

Sensory Regulation

Our sensory system profoundly affects our emotional regulation. Some people are sensory-sensitive (overwhelmed by noise, crowds, texture) while others are sensory-seeking (need stimulation to feel regulated). Understanding your sensory profile helps you design an environment that supports calm and focus.

Meaningful Activity as Medicine

Research shows that engaging in meaningful activity—even brief periods—reduces depression symptoms, increases sense of agency, and activates reward pathways in the brain. What activities make you feel like yourself? These are your therapeutic occupations.

How OT Progress is Monitored

1. **Occupational performance assessment**— Identify 3–5 priority activities you currently struggle with. Rate importance and current performance (1–10). Reassess

every 4–6 weeks.

2. **Routine tracking**– For two weeks, track actual vs. intended daily routine. Gaps reveal where support is needed.
3. **Meaningful activity log**– Each day, note one meaningful activity you engaged in and how it affected your mood. Notice patterns over weeks.
4. **Energy management**– If fatigue or low motivation is a barrier, keep an energy diary. Learn which activities deplete vs. restore you. Build a sustainable daily energy budget.
5. **Environmental audit**– Walk through your home environment. Is it set up to support your routines and recovery? Small environmental modifications (organization, lighting, sensory adjustments) can make significant differences.

29

Authenticity

What Is Authenticity?

Authenticity is the daily practice of letting go of who we think we should be and embracing who we actually are. Researcher Brené Brown, whose work on shame and vulnerability has transformed the field of psychology, describes authenticity not as a personality trait you either have or don't—but as **a collection of choices we make every single day**. It is the choice to show up honestly, to say what you mean, to share what you genuinely feel, and to live in alignment with your values—even when it is uncomfortable and risky to do so.

Brené Brown

"Authenticity is the daily practice of letting go of who we think we should be and embracing who we actually are. Choosing authenticity means cultivating the courage to be imperfect, to set boundaries, and to allow ourselves to be vulnerable."

Why We Hide Our Authentic Selves

Many of us learned early in life that being our true selves was risky. Maybe expressing emotions led to punishment. Maybe being different led to rejection. Maybe vulnerability was used against us. In response, we developed a **false self**—a performed version of ourselves designed to be acceptable to others. Over time, this performance becomes exhausting, and we lose touch with who we actually are beneath it.

Key reasons people hide their authentic selves:

- Fear of rejection ("If they see the real me, they won't like me")
- Fear of judgment or criticism
- Internalized shame about aspects of identity
- Social and cultural pressure to conform
- History of vulnerability being used as a weapon against them
- Perfectionism (the authentic self is imperfect)
- People-pleasing as a coping mechanism

The Cost of Inauthenticity

Living inauthentically is deeply costly—even when it feels safe. The costs include:

- Chronic exhaustion from maintaining a performance
- Difficulty knowing what you genuinely want or feel
- Feeling hollow even within relationships, because the relationship is with your mask—not you
- Resentment when others don't acknowledge the real you

(that they were never shown)

- Depression and anxiety—the body and mind rebel against sustained inauthenticity
- The specific loneliness of being surrounded by people but feeling entirely alone

The Elements of Authenticity

1. Self-Awareness

Knowing who you actually are—your values, your preferences, your feelings, your triggers, your needs—beyond what others expect of you.

2. Courage

The willingness to be seen. To share an unpopular opinion. To say "I'm struggling." To show up imperfectly. Brown traces the word "courage" to its Latin root: *cor*, meaning heart. Authenticity requires the courage to lead with your whole heart.

3. Values Alignment

Living in ways that match what you actually believe in, even when it is costly. When our behavior consistently contradicts our values, we experience a deep dissonance that erodes mental health.

4. Vulnerability

Authenticity is impossible without vulnerability—the willingness to be seen without armor. Brown's research shows that vulnerability is not weakness; it is the birthplace of love, belonging, joy, courage, empathy, and creativity.

5. Letting Go of "Who You Should Be"

Every person carries a set of "should be" scripts—often absorbed from family, culture, religion, or social media. Authenticity requires continuously examining these scripts and choosing which ones you genuinely endorse versus which ones you've simply inherited.

Example of Authenticity in Action

At a dinner party, someone asks Sam how work is going. Sam's instinct is to say "Great!"—the safe, performative answer. But Sam has been struggling significantly. Authentically, Sam says: "Honestly, it's been really tough lately. I'm working through some things." This small act of authenticity opens a genuine conversation and deepens connection.

How to Monitor & Cultivate Authenticity

1. **Values clarification exercise**— List your top 10 values. Then circle the 3 most core. Ask: "Does my life, my relationships, and my daily choices actually reflect these values?" Note the gaps.
2. **Authenticity audit**— Each week, note one moment you were genuine and one moment you performed or hid. What was the difference in how you felt?

3. **Practice micro-vulnerability**— Once per week, share something true about yourself with someone trustworthy that you would normally keep hidden. Start small. Build the tolerance for being seen.
4. **Track the "false self" triggers**— Notice which people, environments, or topics activate your "performed self" most strongly. These are worth exploring in therapy—they often connect to shame and core beliefs.
5. **Notice congruence in your body**— When you are being authentic, your body generally feels open, grounded, and energized. When performing, it often feels tight, anxious, or hollow. Use your body as a congruence meter.

30

Hope

Redefining Hope

Culture defines hope as a passive feeling—a pleasant wish that things might improve, the light at the end of the tunnel. Research tells us something different and far more empowering: hope is an active, learnable cognitive skill—a way of thinking that can be deliberately developed and strengthened, even in the darkest circumstances.

Psychologist Charles Snyder, who developed Hope Theory, defines hope as "a positive motivational state based on an interactively derived sense of successful agency and pathways thinking." In plain language: hope is the combination of having goals, believing you can find a way to reach them, and believing you have the energy and capability to walk that path.

× *Cultural Definition*

- A feeling things will improve
- Passive wishing
- Optimistic naivety
- "The first step toward disappointment"
- Something you either have or don't

✓ *Research Definition*

- An active cognitive skill
- Learnable and developable
- Realistic—acknowledges obstacles
- Goal-directed with pathways thinking
- Stronger predictor of achievement than intelligence

The Three Components of Hope (Snyder's Hope Theory)

1. Goals

Hope requires something to move toward—a goal that is valued, attainable (though not necessarily easy), and specific enough to direct behavior. Without goals, there is nothing for hope to attach to. The goal can be small: "I want to get through this week." Or large: "I want to rebuild my relationship with my children." Both provide the anchoring function that hope needs.

2. Pathways Thinking

The ability to generate multiple routes toward the goal—to see that if one path is blocked, there are others. People with high hope don't give up when the first approach fails; they pivot. This is fundamentally different from optimism, which simply expects success. Pathways thinking is more like being a creative problem-solver: "If that won't work, what else might?"

3. Agency Thinking

The motivational component—the belief in your own capacity to begin and sustain movement along the pathway toward your goal. This is "I can do this" energy. It is not about certainty of success, but about confidence in your own resourcefulness and persistence.

Hope in Action

Riley is in recovery from depression and sets a goal to reconnect with friends. The first path (calling someone) feels too hard. Pathways thinking: "What if I sent a text first? Or what if I went to a group where I didn't have to be 'on'?" Agency thinking: "I've made changes before. I got through last month. I can try one small step today." This is hope as a skill—not a feeling that magically appears, but a set of mental moves that can be practiced.

Hope vs. Optimism

Both involve a positive orientation toward the future. The difference is subtle but important. Optimism is an attitude that things will generally work out—the optimist expects good outcomes. Hope is more realistic and active: the hopeful person acknowledges that things may not work out as planned, yet maintains positive expectancy toward meaningful possibilities while generating pathways to pursue them. Hope can survive disappointment in a way that brittle optimism cannot.

Barriers to Hope

Because hope is fundamentally cognitive, the main barriers are negative thought patterns that tell us goals are impossible or we are incapable:

- Learned helplessness—"Nothing I do makes a difference"
- Schema-driven beliefs—"People like me don't succeed"
- Depression—which reduces both energy and pathway generation
- Past trauma—that has associated striving with danger or failure
- Chronic negative self-talk that undermines agency

How to Monitor & Build Hope

1. **Set one small, concrete goal each week**— Small, achievable goals build the "hope muscle." Each small success genuinely increases hope for larger goals. Write

the goal down.

2. **Practice pathways brainstorming—** For any goal, write down 3 different ways you could approach it. When one path is blocked, return to the list.
3. **Challenge hopeless thoughts—** When you hear "It's pointless," "Nothing will change," ask: "What is the evidence for this? Has anything ever changed in my life before? What would be one small step?"
4. **Build your "evidence for hope" file—** Keep a running list of times you overcame difficulty, made progress, or surprised yourself. Read it when hope feels low.
5. **Track Snyder's Hope Scale—** Available online. Take it monthly. Rising scores reflect genuine hope development over time.

31

Unhealthy Relationships

Understanding Unhealthy Relationship Dynamics

Unhealthy relationships exist on a spectrum—from mildly problematic patterns to outright abuse. Most unhealthy relationships do not begin that way. They often start with genuine connection, warmth, and even the feeling of being "finally understood." Over time, however, certain patterns emerge that erode safety, autonomy, and self-worth. Understanding these patterns is essential for protecting yourself and making informed choices about your relationships.

An important truth: many people who grew up in homes with unhealthy relationship dynamics internalized those patterns as "normal." What feels familiar is not always what is healthy. Recognizing unhealthy patterns often requires learning to see what you were conditioned not to see.

The Warning Signs: Red Flags

Control & Coercion

- Monitoring your location, phone, social media, or finances
- Isolating you from friends and family ("They're a bad influence")
- Making all the major decisions without genuine input from you
- Threatening negative consequences if you don't comply
- Demanding to know where you are at all times

Disrespect & Contempt

- Name-calling, insults, put-downs—even framed as "jokes"
- Eye-rolling, sighing, or mocking when you share feelings
- Dismissing your opinions or feelings as stupid or overreacting
- Contempt (Gottman's #1 predictor of relationship failure)

Manipulation

- **Gaslighting:** Making you question your own memory, perception, or sanity. ("That never happened." "You're too sensitive." "You're imagining things.")
- **DARVO:** Deny, Attack, Reverse Victim and Offender—the perpetrator claims to be the real victim when confronted
- **Love bombing:** Overwhelming affection early in a relationship to create rapid attachment, followed by withdrawal or control
- **Guilt-tripping:** Using guilt to control behavior ("After

everything I've done for you...")
- **Silent treatment:** Withdrawing communication as punishment

The Cycle of Abuse

Many abusive relationships follow a predictable cycle:

1. **Tension building**—Walking on eggshells. Tension escalates.
2. **Incident**—An explosion of abuse (physical, emotional, verbal)
3. **Reconciliation ("Honeymoon")**—Apologies, affection, promises to change, gifts
4. **Calm**—Things seem normal. The incident is minimized or forgotten.
5. Back to #1—The cycle repeats, often escalating over time.

Example of Gaslighting

After a partner yells and throws an object, they later say: "I never yelled at you. You're always so dramatic. You push my buttons and then act like you're the victim." Over time, the target begins to doubt their own perception and may come to believe the distorted version of events.

Why People Stay

Staying in an unhealthy relationship is not a sign of weakness or stupidity. People stay for deeply complex reasons:

- Fear of physical retaliation if they leave

- Financial dependence or practical entrapment
- Hope that it will return to the way it was (love for the good parts)
- Trauma bonding—a powerful attachment formed through alternating abuse and affection
- Children or family pressure
- Shame and not wanting others to know
- Core schemas that make this feel like what love is supposed to feel like

How to Monitor & Move Toward Safety

1. **Safety first**— If you are in physical danger, contact the National Domestic Violence Hotline (1-800-799-7233) or a local shelter before any other step. Safety planning with a professional is essential.
2. **Name the pattern**— Write down specific incidents, dates, and patterns. This helps cut through gaslighting and creates clarity. Your reality is real.
3. **Rebuild your support network**— If isolation has occurred, begin slowly reconnecting with one trusted person outside the relationship.
4. **Explore the attachment**— With a therapist, explore why this dynamic feels familiar or compelling. What schemas might make this relationship feel like home?
5. **Create a safety plan**— Even if you are not ready to leave, have a plan: trusted contact, essential documents location, emergency funds if possible. Having a plan reduces helplessness.

32

Trust

What Is Trust?

Trust is the willingness to be vulnerable with someone—to rely on them and believe that they will not exploit or harm that vulnerability. Trust is not a binary switch (you either trust someone or you don't). It is a complex, multi-dimensional experience that exists in degrees and across different domains. You might trust someone to keep a secret but not to be on time; to be loyal but not to be emotionally available.

Trust is also relational—it is built or eroded through specific, repeated behaviors over time. It cannot be demanded or forced. It is earned through consistent, reliable, aligned action.

The BRAVING Acronym (Brené Brown)

Brené Brown identified 7 components of trust through her research, summarized in the acronym BRAVING:

- **B—Boundaries:** You respect my boundaries when I set them, and when you're unsure, you ask. You are willing to say no.
- **R—Reliability:** You do what you say you will do. You keep your commitments, are aware of your limitations, and don't over-promise.
- **A—Accountability:** You own your mistakes, apologize, and make amends. You don't expect me to just "get over it."
- **V—Vault:** You don't share information or experiences that are not yours to share. You treat my confidences as sacred.
- **I—Integrity:** You choose courage over comfort. You choose what is right over what is fun, fast, or easy. You live your stated values.
- **N—Non-judgment:** I can ask for what I need. I can talk about how I'm feeling. I can tell my truth without fear of judgment from you.
- **G—Generosity:** You extend the most generous interpretation possible to my intentions, words, and actions.

Rebuilding Trust After Betrayal

Betrayal—whether through infidelity, broken confidences, lies, or abandonment—is one of the most painful relational experiences. Gottman's research offers a framework called **Atone, Attune, Attach** for rebuilding trust after betrayal:

Phase 1: Atone

The person who broke trust takes full responsibility. There is no blame-shifting, no minimizing, no "but you did X too." A genuine, specific apology that acknowledges the impact on the other person is the foundation. This phase also requires transparency and the ending of any ongoing harmful behavior.

Phase 2: Attune

The couple or individuals work toward genuine understanding of what led to the betrayal—not to excuse it, but to understand the context and feelings. Both people must be willing to hear difficult truths about what each person needed that wasn't being met. This requires empathy and emotional engagement.

Phase 3: Attach

Gradually, through sustained consistent behavior over time, a new form of security is established. This is not the naïve trust of before—it is a more mature, eyes-open trust built on demonstrated reliability and accountability.

Self-Trust

Often overlooked, self-trust is foundational to trusting others. Self-trust means believing in your own perceptions, judgment, values, and capabilities. Many people who grew up in invalidating environments or trauma have had their self-trust systematically eroded. They doubt their own feelings, question their own reality, and override their own instincts. Rebuilding self-trust is often the beginning of the ability to build healthy trust with others.

Signs of Low Self-Trust

Constantly second-guessing your own decisions. Seeking excessive reassurance from others. Overriding your gut feelings in relationships. Staying in situations that feel wrong because you doubt your own read. Believing others know what's best for you better than you do.

How to Monitor & Build Trust

1. **BRAVING inventory**– Rate each of the 7 BRAVING elements in your key relationships (1–10). Which elements are strongest? Which need work? Have an honest conversation from this assessment.
2. **Track micro-moments of trust**– Gottman notes that trust is built in small moments. Keep a log of times trust was honored or broken in small interactions. Notice patterns.
3. **Build self-trust first**– Daily, practice making one decision and honoring it. Practice saying one thing you genuinely believe, even if it's uncomfortable. Notice what your gut is saying and acknowledge it.
4. **Post-betrayal pacing**– If rebuilding after betrayal, resist the pressure to "just forgive and move on." Trust rebuilding takes consistent behavior over months or years. Progress is measured in sustained reliability, not declarations.
5. **Work with a therapist**– especially if trust was sig-

nificantly damaged early in life. Therapy is itself an experience of a trustworthy relationship that can rewire trust expectations over time.

33

Boundaries

What Are Boundaries?

Boundaries are the limits you set to protect your physical, emotional, mental, and spiritual well-being in relationships. They define what you are and are not willing to accept, what you will and will not do, and how you expect to be treated. Boundaries are not walls (which shut everyone out) or punishment (which try to control others). They are **clear definitions of your own limits, communicated with respect**.

A crucial distinction: **boundaries are about what YOU will do, not what you demand others do.** "You must stop calling me at midnight" is a demand. "If you continue calling at midnight, I will turn my phone off at 10pm" is a boundary. You can only control your own behavior—not others'.

The Purpose of Boundaries

Boundaries are not about keeping people out. They are about defining the conditions under which you can remain in relationship without resentment, harm, or loss of self. Paradoxically, healthy boundaries make intimacy safer and deeper.

Types of Boundaries

Physical Boundaries

Your body, personal space, and physical privacy. Who can touch you, how, and when. Whether someone can enter your room or go through your belongings. Physical boundaries protect your bodily autonomy and safety.

Emotional Boundaries

Protecting your emotional well-being and separating your feelings from others'. You are not responsible for others' emotions. Others are not responsible for yours (though they are responsible for how they treat you). Emotional boundaries prevent you from absorbing others' distress as your own, or from having your feelings dismissed, manipulated, or weaponized.

Mental / Intellectual Boundaries

Your right to your own thoughts, beliefs, opinions, and values—even when they differ from others. No one has the right to tell you what to think or to relentlessly argue you out of your own perspectives.

Time Boundaries

Your right to manage your own time. Saying no to requests that overextend you. Protecting time for rest, priorities, and your own needs. "I can't help you move on Saturday—I have a prior commitment to myself."

Sexual Boundaries

Your right to determine what sexual activity you participate in, with whom, when, and how. No means no. Enthusiastic consent is the standard.

Material/Financial Boundaries

What you will and will not share, loan, or contribute financially. These often require explicit communication because people have vastly different assumptions about money and sharing.

Why Setting Boundaries Is Hard

- **Fear of anger:** "If I say no, they'll be furious and I can't handle that"
- **Fear of abandonment:** "If I have limits, they'll leave"
- **Guilt:** "Setting limits means I'm selfish or unkind"
- **Lack of model:** You never saw healthy boundaries demonstrated
- **People-pleasing schema:** Your worth is tied to making others happy
- **Enmeshment:** Others' feelings and needs genuinely feel

like your own

How to Set a Boundary

1. **Identify the limit:** What specifically is not working for you? What are you feeling that signals a boundary has been or is about to be crossed?
2. **Know your "why":** What need are you protecting? Safety? Energy? Autonomy? Clarity on this helps you hold the boundary when challenged.
3. **State it clearly and simply:** "I'm not comfortable with ____." "I won't be able to ____." "Please don't ____."
4. **Include the consequence:** "If ____ continues, I will ____." (And mean it. Empty consequences undermine all future boundaries.)
5. **Follow through:** The boundary is only real if you enforce it. This is often the hardest part—especially with people who are used to you having no limits.

Example of Setting a Boundary

Situation: Family member calls multiple times per day and becomes critical on the call.

Boundary statement: "I love you and I want to stay connected. I'm able to talk once in the evening—I won't be answering calls during the day. If the conversation becomes critical of my choices, I'll let you know I need to end the call."

When challenged: "I understand you're upset. I still need to go now. Let's talk tomorrow evening."

How to Monitor & Strengthen Your Boundaries

1. **Boundary inventory**— In each significant relationship, identify one area where you feel resentment, exhaustion, or violation. Resentment is almost always a sign that a boundary needs to be set or enforced.
2. **Practice starting small**— Set boundaries in low-stakes situations first. Build confidence before tackling the most difficult relationships.
3. **Track your body's signals**— Notice physical discomfort, tension, or dread before interactions. These are early boundary-crossing signals. Learn to trust them.
4. **Prepare for pushback**— New boundaries often generate resistance, anger, or guilt-tripping from people used to no limits. This is expected and does not mean you are wrong. Prepare for it mentally.
5. **Notice the relief**— After enforcing a boundary (even a difficult one), notice if there is relief alongside the anxiety. This relief is information: you did something right for yourself.

34

Assertiveness

The Three Communication Styles

Every communication choice we make falls somewhere on a spectrum with three key positions. Understanding where you tend to operate—and why—is the first step toward developing genuine assertiveness.

Passive

- Avoids expressing needs or opinions
- Defers to others constantly
- Says yes when meaning no
- Apologizes excessively
- Hopes others will "just know"
- Internal cost: resentment, invisibility, self-abandonment

Aggressive

- Expresses needs at others' expense
- Threatens, dominates, or intimidates
- Interrupts, dismisses others
- Uses "you always/never" accusations
- Wins arguments, loses relationships
- Internal cost: isolation, guilt, escalating conflict

✅ *Assertive (The Middle Path)*

- Expresses needs and feelings clearly and respectfully
- Listens genuinely and acknowledges others' perspectives
- Uses "I" statements rather than "you" accusations
- Says no without excessive apologizing
- Maintains personal boundaries without punishing others
- Aims for mutual respect and understanding

Why We Default Away From Assertiveness

Passivity usually develops from fear of rejection, conflict, or retaliation—often rooted in Subjugation, Abandonment, or Defectiveness schemas. Aggression often develops as an overcorrection to helplessness, or as a pattern modeled in childhood. Assertiveness requires believing two things simultaneously: **"My needs matter" AND "Your needs matter."** If either of those beliefs is missing, assertive communication breaks down.

The Core Tools of Assertive Communication

"I" Statements

The formula: **"I feel [emotion] when [specific behavior] because [impact]. I would like [specific request]."**

Example

Aggressive: "You never listen to me. You always make everything about yourself."

Passive: "It's fine. Don't worry about it." (while seething internally)

Assertive: "I feel dismissed when I'm interrupted while talking, because it makes me feel like what I'm saying isn't important. I'd really appreciate it if you could let me finish my thought."

The Broken Record Technique

When others persist in pushing back on your no, calmly and firmly repeat your position without escalating or defending excessively: "I understand you'd like me to, and I'm not able to." "I hear that this is important to you, and I'm still not going to be able to help with this." Keep the same calm tone and the same message.

DEAR MAN (DBT)

- **D**escribe the situation factually
- **E**xpress your feelings using "I" statements
- **A**ssert your request clearly
- **R**einforce the relationship or mutual benefit
- **M**indful—stay focused on your goal, don't get sidetracked
- **A**ppear confident—tone, posture, eye contact matter
- **N**egotiate—be willing to give something to get something

The Assertive "No"

You have the right to say no without a lengthy explanation or apology. A simple, honest no is more respectful than a resentful yes. Practice: "I'm not going to be able to." (No justification required.) Or, if you'd like to preserve the relationship: "I can't do that, but I could do ___."

How to Monitor & Develop Assertiveness

1. **Assertiveness log**— Each week, note 3 situations where you were passive, aggressive, or assertive. What was the trigger? What did you do? What would assertive look like?
2. **Practice with low-stakes situations first**— Order what you actually want at a restaurant. Ask for what you need in a low-conflict moment. Build assertiveness muscles before the big conversations.
3. **Role-play with a therapist or trusted person**— Rehearse difficult conversations before having them. Notice how your body feels during assertive vs. passive

responses.

4. **Track internal state**— Notice where in your body you feel the pull toward passivity (constriction? a need to disappear?). This is the schema activating. Name it and make a conscious choice about how to proceed.
5. **Celebrate assertive moments**— Each time you express a genuine need, say a clean no, or hold a position calmly, acknowledge it. These are real achievements, especially early on.

35

Stigma

What Is Mental Health Stigma?

Stigma is a mark of disgrace or shame associated with a particular circumstance, quality, or person. Mental health stigma specifically refers to negative attitudes, beliefs, stereotypes, and discrimination directed toward people who have mental health conditions—or directed by those people toward themselves. Stigma is one of the most significant barriers to people seeking and receiving mental health care, and it causes its own profound harm on top of the illness itself.

The CDC identifies three main types of mental health stigma:

Three Types of Stigma

1. Public Stigma

Negative attitudes and beliefs held by the general public about people with mental health conditions. This includes stereotypes (people with mental illness are violent or incompetent), prejudice (agreeing with those stereotypes), and discrimination (acting on that prejudice by, for example, refusing to hire someone or excluding them socially).

Example of Public Stigma

"I'd be nervous hiring someone with bipolar disorder—they're unpredictable." This is a stereotyped belief based on fear, not evidence. In reality, most people with bipolar disorder are not violent and are capable employees—often especially empathetic and creative ones.

2. Self-Stigma

This occurs when a person internalizes the negative messages of public stigma and applies them to themselves. Self-stigma produces deep shame, secrecy, and hopelessness, and it directly reduces a person's motivation to seek help ("I should be able to handle this on my own") and their sense of their own future prospects ("Someone like me can't recover").

Example of Self-Stigma

"I must be weak to have depression. I'm embarrassed to tell anyone or go to therapy—what would they think? People like me just need to toughen up." This internal narrative prevents help-seeking and compounds suffering.

3. Structural Stigma

Policies, laws, and institutional practices that disadvantage people with mental health conditions—such as inadequate insurance coverage for mental health treatment, discrimination in housing or employment, or a legal system that treats mental illness as a moral failure rather than a health condition.

The Impact of Stigma

- Delays in seeking treatment—the average delay between symptom onset and first treatment is **11 years**, largely due to stigma
- Poorer treatment outcomes due to incomplete disclosure with providers
- Social isolation and loneliness
- Reduced employment opportunities
- Internalized hopelessness about recovery
- Physical health impacts from stress and delayed care
- Increased risk of suicide

Dismantling Stigma: What Works

Education

The most effective approach to reducing public stigma is **contact + education**—personal stories from people with mental health conditions, combined with accurate information that replaces myths with facts.

Language Matters

- Say "person with schizophrenia" not "a schizophrenic" (person-first language)
- Say "died by suicide" not "committed suicide" (the word "committed" implies crime)
- Avoid words like "crazy," "psycho," "nuts" as casual insults

Overcoming Self-Stigma

- Challenge the internal stigmatizing beliefs as you would any cognitive distortion
- Connect with others who share your experience—peer support dismantles isolation
- Remember: mental health conditions are medical conditions, not character flaws
- Seek treatment without shame—you would not be ashamed to treat diabetes

How to Monitor & Counter Stigma

1. **Identify your own stigmatizing beliefs**— Honestly examine what you believe about mental illness, your own condition, and people who go to therapy. Challenge each belief with evidence.
2. **Track self-stigma moments**— Each week, note times you felt ashamed of your mental health. What triggered it? What message did you tell yourself? Challenge it: "Would I say this about someone with diabetes?"
3. **Practice disclosure selectively**— Telling your story, even once, to someone safe begins to erode self-stigma's

power. You don't have to tell everyone—but telling someone is powerful.

4. **Become educated**— Reading accurate information about your condition and recovery rates combats hopelessness driven by stigma. Recovery is far more common than stigma suggests.
5. **Advocate when able**— In small ways—correcting misinformation, using accurate language, supporting mental health awareness—advocacy reduces stigma and builds empowerment.

36

Symptom Management

What Is Symptom Management?

Symptom management refers to the evidence-based strategies, tools, and practices that help reduce the intensity, frequency, and impact of mental health symptoms on your daily life. It is not about eliminating the presence of symptoms—that is often an unrealistic goal, especially early in recovery. It is about building a toolbox of skills and supports that allow you to function, engage meaningfully with your life, and gradually reduce the symptoms' hold over you.

Good symptom management is both **proactive** (building wellness practices that prevent or buffer against symptoms) and **reactive** (skills for when symptoms escalate).

Tier 1: The Wellness Foundation

Research consistently shows that these biological basics have a profound impact on mental health symptoms—often as powerful as medication or therapy alone:

Sleep

Sleep is the brain's primary maintenance and emotional regulation system. Chronic sleep deprivation dramatically worsens anxiety, depression, irritability, and cognitive function. Sleep hygiene practices include: consistent sleep/wake times, no screens 60 minutes before bed, cool/dark/quiet environment, no caffeine after 2pm, brief relaxation practice before sleep.

Nutrition

The gut-brain connection is real and significant. Blood sugar instability produces mood instability. Anti-inflammatory diets (rich in vegetables, whole grains, omega-3s) are associated with lower rates of depression and anxiety. Regular, balanced meals maintain the neurochemical baseline needed for emotional regulation.

Movement

Exercise is one of the most potent antidepressants and anxiolytics available—with no prescription required. 30 minutes of moderate aerobic activity 5 days/week produces neurochemical changes equivalent to antidepressants for mild to moderate depression. Even a 10-minute walk has measurable immediate effects on mood.

Connection

Social isolation is a major driver and amplifier of mental health symptoms. Regular, genuine human connection is a biological need. Even brief positive social contact activates the parasympathetic nervous system and releases oxytocin—both of which directly reduce symptom intensity.

Tier 2: Active Coping Skills

Distress Tolerance (DBT)

- **TIP:** Temperature (cold water on face), Intense exercise, Paced breathing
- **TIPP:** Above + Progressive muscle relaxation
- **ACCEPTS:** Activities, Contributing, Comparisons, Emotions (opposite), Pushing away, Thoughts, Sensations—ways to survive crisis without making it worse
- **Self-soothe with 5 senses:** Create a "soothing kit" with items that comfort each sense

Grounding Techniques

- 5-4-3-2-1 sensory grounding
- Cold water on wrists or face
- Holding ice
- Slow, rhythmic movement
- Naming objects in the room

- Orienting statements: "I am [name]. Today is [date]. I am in [location]. I am safe."

Tier 3: Professional Support

- **Medication:** When appropriate, psychiatric medication can be a crucial tool—not a crutch or a failure
- **Individual therapy:** Regular sessions provide ongoing support, skill-building, and processing of difficult material
- **Support groups:** Peer support reduces isolation, normalizes struggle, and provides practical wisdom
- **Crisis planning:** Having a documented plan for high-distress moments reduces their danger significantly

Your Personal Crisis Safety Plan

Every person managing mental health symptoms should have a written safety plan that includes:

1. Warning signs that a crisis may be developing
2. Internal coping strategies (things I can do alone)
3. People and settings that provide distraction
4. People I can ask for help (name, number)
5. Professional crisis contacts (therapist, crisis line, ER)
6. Ways to make the environment safer during a crisis

How to Monitor Symptom Management Progress

1. **Symptom tracking**— Rate your primary symptoms daily (1–10). Track over weeks to identify patterns: What triggers spikes? What reduces them? Which skills help most?
2. **Wellness check-in**— Each Sunday, assess: How did I sleep? Eat? Move? Connect socially? Which areas were neglected? Set one realistic intention for the week.
3. **Skill practice log**— Note each time you use a coping skill. What was the symptom level before and after? Build an evidence base for which skills work for you.
4. **Celebrate stability**— Stability is progress. If symptoms haven't worsened even in a difficult week, that is a genuine achievement worth acknowledging.
5. **Review and update your crisis plan annually**— and after any significant life change or mental health crisis.

37

Co-Dependency

What Is Co-Dependency?

Co-dependency is a pattern of behavior in which a person excessively relies on another person for their sense of identity, worth, and emotional well-being—or in which a person's life becomes organized primarily around managing, fixing, or enabling another person's behavior. Originally identified in the context of relationships with people struggling with addiction, co-dependency has since been recognized as a broader relational pattern that can appear in any close relationship.

At its core, co-dependency is a loss of self. The co-dependent person's needs, feelings, desires, and identity become so enmeshed with those of another that they genuinely lose track of where they end and the other person begins. This creates a profound sense of emptiness, resentment, and powerlessness—alongside a paradoxical inability to disengage from the very relationships that are harming them.

Signs of Co-Dependency

- Excessive preoccupation with the thoughts, feelings, and behaviors of another person
- Difficulty identifying and expressing your own needs, feelings, and opinions
- Compulsive caretaking—feeling responsible for others' emotions and choices
- Difficulty saying no, setting limits, or tolerating others' disappointment
- Deriving self-worth entirely from being needed by others
- Feeling guilty when you take time for yourself
- Minimizing your own needs and chronic self-sacrifice
- Fear of abandonment driving extreme compliance
- Enabling—protecting others from the natural consequences of their choices
- Chronic resentment—giving more than you have, then resenting it
- Believing your love or caretaking can "fix" or change another person

The Core Dynamic

Co-dependency is not love, even though it feels like love. It is a form of control driven by fear—the fear that if you don't manage, fix, or care for the other person, you will be abandoned, or they will fall apart, or you will be revealed as unworthy. Love, by contrast, allows the other person to be responsible for themselves.

The Origins of Co-Dependency

Co-dependency typically develops in families where:

- One or more members had addiction, chronic illness, or mental health challenges
- Emotions were not discussed, were minimized, or were dangerous to express
- A child was required to take on adult emotional responsibilities (parentification)
- Love and approval were conditional on meeting the parent's needs
- The child learned that their worth came from being helpful, quiet, or compliant

Recovery from Co-Dependency

Step 1: Recognition

The first step is recognizing the pattern without shame. Co-dependency developed as a survival strategy in an environment where it was necessary. It is not a character flaw—it is a learned adaptation that has outlived its usefulness.

Step 2: Reconnecting with Self

Learning to ask and answer: What do I feel? What do I need? What do I want? What do I think?—independently of what others feel/need/want/think. This often requires deliberate practice, as the capacity may have atrophied significantly.

Step 3: Detachment (with love)

Al-Anon's concept of "detachment with love" means releasing the compulsive need to fix, manage, or protect others from their own experiences—while remaining genuinely caring. You can love someone deeply and still allow them to face the consequences of their own choices.

Step 4: Building the Self

Developing interests, relationships, values, and activities that belong to you—not in service of another person. Building the experience of your own independent existence as valuable and meaningful.

How to Monitor & Recover from Co-Dependency

1. **Self-check daily**— "Whose feelings am I carrying today? What do I actually need right now?" Start small—even answering "What do I want for breakfast" autonomously is practice.
2. **Track enabling behavior**— When did you protect someone from their own consequences this week? What were you afraid would happen if you didn't? What might healthy allowing look like?
3. **Attend Al-Anon, CoDA (Co-Dependents Anonymous), or a therapy group**— Peer support with others in recovery is uniquely effective.
4. **Practice receiving**— Allow others to care for you. Notice the discomfort. Practice tolerating receiving without immediately deflecting or giving back.

5. **Build your identity outside the relationship—** Set aside time weekly for something that is entirely yours: a hobby, a friendship, a spiritual practice, a creative pursuit.

38

Dependency

Understanding Dependency

Dependency is a normal and unavoidable aspect of human existence. We are inherently relational beings—wired, neurologically and evolutionarily, to need others. Healthy dependency is the ability to lean on others appropriately, to ask for help, to accept care, and to rely on others without losing yourself in the process. It becomes problematic only when it exceeds what is appropriate, reasonable, or healthy for all involved.

One of the most common and damaging myths in Western culture is that needing others is a sign of weakness—that the ideal person is entirely self-sufficient. This belief drives people toward isolation, prevents help-seeking, and creates shame around the very normal human need for connection and support.

Healthy Dependency vs. Unhealthy Dependency

Healthy Dependency

- Asking for help when you genuinely need it
- Relying on a few trusted people for emotional support
- Accepting care without feeling shame
- Being able to function independently when alone
- Knowing you also have internal resources
- Dependency that is mutual and reciprocal

Unhealthy Dependency

- Inability to make decisions without others' approval
- Relying on one person for all emotional needs
- Inability to tolerate being alone
- Seeking constant reassurance
- Allowing others to define your reality and worth
- Paralysis without a particular person present

The Dependence/Incompetence Schema

One of the 18 Early Maladaptive Schemas specifically addresses unhealthy dependency—the core belief that one is fundamentally unable to handle everyday responsibilities without significant help. People with this schema may:

- Defer all decisions to others—a partner, parent, boss, or therapist
- Experience intense anxiety when required to act independently
- Seek constant reassurance before acting
- Attribute their successes to luck or others' help, and their

failures to their own incompetence
- Avoid situations that would require them to demonstrate self-sufficiency

This schema typically develops in families where the child was overprotected, never allowed to fail or struggle, or where parents modeled extreme helplessness. The child never developed the internal confidence that comes from successfully navigating challenges independently.

Building Healthy Dependence

The goal is not to need no one—that is impossible and unhealthy. The goal is to **rely on others from a position of choice and strength, not fear and desperation**. This requires building internal resources and a network of trusted people simultaneously:

- Identify the internal resources you actually do have (and have used before)
- Gradually expand your tolerance for independent action through small challenges
- Build a diverse support network rather than depending entirely on one person
- Practice asking for help as a choice, not as desperation
- Allow yourself to experience successful independent action—this is how internal confidence builds

How to Monitor & Develop Healthy Dependency

1. **Dependency mapping**— Who do you depend on for what? Is your dependency network diverse? Is there any one person carrying too much of your relational weight?
2. **Practice one independent action per week**— Something you would normally defer to someone else. Note how it feels before (anxiety) and after (hopefully, some pride or relief).
3. **Challenge incompetence beliefs**— Keep a log of things you successfully handled independently. This builds a genuine evidence base against the dependency schema.
4. **Practice asking for help as a choice**— Before calling on support, ask: "Is this something I genuinely need help with, or am I avoiding the discomfort of doing it myself?" Then make a conscious choice.
5. **Notice progress in tolerating aloneness**— Can you sit with yourself for increasing periods without needing to contact someone or distract? This tolerance is a marker of growing internal security.

39

Independency

What Is Independence?

Independence is the capacity to think, feel, act, and function from one's own internal resources—to have a stable sense of self, to make decisions aligned with personal values, to regulate emotions, and to meet one's own needs without requiring constant external validation or support. It is a developmental achievement and a lifelong practice.

True independence is not the absence of need for others—that is isolation, which is harmful. True independence is the internal capacity to be with oneself, to trust one's own judgment, and to function effectively—while remaining genuinely open to relationships, connection, and support. It is being alone without being lonely; being self-directed without being rigidly closed.

Important Distinction

Pseudo-independence—the performance of not needing anyone, often driven by mistrust, trauma, or shame—is not true independence. True independence knows it can lean on others when needed. Pseudo-independence cannot.

Components of Healthy Independence

1. Autonomous Decision-Making

The ability to make decisions based on your own values, desires, and judgment—not primarily out of fear of others' reactions or need for their approval. This includes the ability to make decisions and tolerate uncertainty about whether they were "right."

2. Self-Regulation

The ability to manage your own emotional states without requiring another person to calm, reassure, or manage you. This does not mean never seeking comfort—it means having internal tools available when others are not.

3. Personal Identity

A clear sense of who you are—your values, preferences, opinions, history, and goals—that does not shift fundamentally depending on who you are with. You can adapt your communication style without losing your core self.

4. Self-Sufficiency in Daily Functioning

The practical ability to manage your own life: finances, health care, home, work, and social connections. Being able to meet your own basic needs without requiring another person to manage them for you (within reasonable life circumstances).

5. Healthy Solitude

The ability to spend time alone and derive genuine rest, pleasure, or meaning from it. Solitude is different from loneliness: loneliness is painful disconnection; solitude is chosen, renewing aloneness. The capacity for healthy solitude is a marker of solid internal independence.

When Independence Becomes a Problem

For some people—especially those with attachment trauma or Mistrust/Abuse schemas—independence becomes exaggerated into **compulsive self-reliance**: a rigid refusal to need anyone, accept help, or show vulnerability. This is actually a coping mode (the Detached Protector), not true independence. Indicators include:

- Pride in "never needing anyone"
- Discomfort with receiving help, care, or attention
- Dismissal of the need for therapy or support ("I can handle my own problems")
- Relationships consistently kept at arm's length
- Internal aloneness even in relationships

How to Monitor & Build Healthy Independence

1. **Values clarification**— What do you actually value, independent of what others expect of you? List 10 things you genuinely enjoy, believe, or care about. This is the

bedrock of independent identity.

2. **Practice autonomous decision-making**— Make 3 decisions this week without consulting anyone first. Small decisions are fine. Notice how it feels to trust yourself.
3. **Build solitude tolerance gradually**— If being alone triggers anxiety, start with 10 minutes of intentional solitude per day. Gradually extend. What do you notice when with only yourself?
4. **Journal your own opinions**— Before discussing a topic with someone whose opinion you value greatly, write your own position first. Notice how much (or little) it shifts after conversation.
5. **Track self-regulation moments**— Each time you manage a difficult emotion using internal resources (breathing, grounding, journaling) rather than immediate external reassurance, note it. This builds confidence in your own capacity.

40

Interdependency

The Highest Form of Human Connection

Interdependency is the balance point between dependence and independence—and it is the hallmark of the healthiest human relationships. Interdependent people are both autonomous individuals and deeply connected partners. They can rely on each other without losing themselves; they can be vulnerable without being engulfed; they can support each other without becoming responsible for each other.

Interdependency sits in the center of a spectrum. On one end: unhealthy dependence (enmeshment, co-dependency, loss of self). On the other end: unhealthy independence (isolation, compulsive self-reliance, emotional unavailability). Interdependency holds both ends in creative tension.

The Paradox of Interdependency

The more solidly yourself you are—the stronger your sense of personal identity and self-worth—the more freely and completely you can love another person. Security in oneself is not the enemy of intimacy. It is the foundation of it.

Characteristics of Interdependent Relationships

- **Mutual support**—Both people care for and receive care from each other; the balance flows back and forth over time
- **Maintained individuality**—Both people have their own interests, friendships, goals, and identities that are respected and encouraged
- **Healthy communication**—Needs, feelings, and limits are expressed openly and received with respect
- **Mutual responsibility**—Each person is responsible for their own emotional regulation, behaviors, and choices
- **Secure base and safe haven**—The relationship provides both the safety to rest and the confidence to explore the world
- **Ability to disagree**—Conflict is navigated without threatening the relationship's fundamental security
- **Choosing, not needing**—The relationship is based on genuine desire for each other's company and love—not on fear of being alone or need for rescue

Interdependency vs. Co-Dependency: Key Differences

Co-Dependency

- Self-worth contingent on the other
- Difficulty functioning independently
- Other's emotions feel like your responsibility
- Fear drives the relationship
- Identity merges—"we" replaces "I"
- Staying even when harmful

Interdependency

- Self-worth is internally grounded
- Both can function independently
- Empathy without taking over
- Choice drives the relationship
- Both "we" AND "I" are honored
- Staying because it is genuinely good

Building Interdependency

Interdependency is not a destination you arrive at—it is a dynamic practice. It requires:

- Ongoing development of your own independent self (interests, values, identity, self-regulation)
- Ongoing vulnerability—continuing to let people in rather than self-protecting
- Regular, honest communication about needs, limits, and experiences
- Willingness to allow others to be themselves—including when their choices differ from yours
- Repair skills—the ability to reconnect after rupture without catastrophizing

Interdependency in Action

Alex and Sam are partners. Alex is going through a difficult period at work. Sam provides support and listens. But Sam also maintains their own social life, hobbies, and emotional health—they do not become Alex's therapist or abandon their own needs to manage Alex's crisis. When Sam is struggling a few months later, Alex is there. The relationship flows. Both remain themselves. Both are genuinely there for each other.

How to Monitor & Cultivate Interdependency

1. **Relationship balance check**– Is this relationship genuinely mutual over time? Does both people's wellbeing matter equally? Is there space for both individuality AND togetherness?
2. **Dual identity practice**– Each week, invest in something that is entirely yours AND something that belongs to the relationship. Both need attention.
3. **Ask without demanding**– Practice requesting support: "I'm struggling and I could use help. Are you in a good space for that right now?"–honoring both your need AND the other person's capacity.
4. **Hold your own emotions**– Practice being with difficult emotions for a period before reaching out. This builds tolerance and prevents the relationship from being your only regulation tool.
5. **Celebrate each other's independence**– Actively encourage and celebrate your partner's or friend's independent pursuits, even when it means less time together. This is a practice of genuine love over fear.

41

Grief & Loss

What Is Grief?

Grief is the natural and necessary response to loss. It is not a disorder, a weakness, or something to be overcome as quickly as possible. Grief is the process through which we integrate loss into our lives—through which we find a way to carry forward what and whom we have loved while continuing to live and grow. It is one of the most profound human experiences, and one of the most misunderstood.

Loss comes in many forms—and grief is appropriate for all of them:

- Death of a loved one, pet, or pregnancy
- End of a significant relationship (divorce, friendship ending)
- Loss of health, functioning, or physical ability
- Loss of a job, career, or financial security
- Loss of a home, community, or sense of belonging
- Loss of identity (the person you thought you were)

- Loss of safety (through trauma or abuse)
- Loss of a future you expected (infertility, a diagnosis)
- Disenfranchised grief—losses that are not publicly recognized (pregnancy loss, loss of an estranged person, loss of a past relationship)

The Stages of Grief (Kübler-Ross)

Elisabeth Kübler-Ross's stage model is the most widely known framework. It is important to understand: these stages are not linear, not universal, and not meant to be "completed" in sequence. They are descriptions of emotional experiences that may occur, in any order, repeatedly, and with varying intensity.

- **Denial:** "This can't be happening." A natural initial buffer against overwhelming reality. "She's just in the hospital—she'll be back."
- **Anger:** "Why is this happening? Who is to blame?" Anger at the situation, at others, at God, at yourself. An important and necessary part of grief.
- **Bargaining:** "If only I had... What if I had done..." The mind searching for a way to undo the loss. "If only I'd made them go to the doctor sooner."
- **Depression:** Deep sadness, withdrawal, fatigue, hopelessness. The full weight of the loss settling in. This is grief doing its work—not a disorder to be fixed immediately.
- **Acceptance:** Not "being okay" with the loss, but finding a way to acknowledge its reality and continue living. "This happened. I will carry it. I will also live."

Complicated Grief (Prolonged Grief Disorder)

For most people, grief naturally softens over time—not disappearing, but becoming more integrated. For some, grief remains overwhelmingly intense for months or years, significantly impairing daily functioning. This is called **prolonged grief disorder** (formerly complicated grief) and is a clinical condition that responds well to specialized therapy:

- Persistent, intense longing for the person/situation lost—beyond expected cultural norms
- Difficulty accepting the reality of the loss
- Feeling that part of oneself has died along with the loss
- Inability to trust others or engage in meaningful activities
- Bitterness or anger related to the loss that does not diminish
- Feeling that life is meaningless without the deceased

Moving Through Grief: What Actually Helps

Allow Rather Than Resist

Grief cannot be outrun, intellectualized, or numbed away permanently. What is suppressed does not disappear—it waits. Creating deliberate space to feel the grief—to cry, to remember, to miss—is not weakness. It is the process itself.

Honor the Loss

Rituals matter—whether traditional (funerals, memorial services) or personal (writing letters to what was lost, creating a memory box, maintaining a meaningful tradition). Rituals create structure for grief and honor what was real and important.

Maintain Connection

Research by grief scholar William Worden suggests the goal of grief is not to "let go" but to **find a new way to hold on**—to maintain a continuing bond with what was lost while also re-engaging with life. This might mean keeping a photo, talking about a deceased loved one, or honoring their values in how you live.

Seek Support

Grief shared is grief lightened. Whether through trusted friends, family, support groups (hospice grief groups, grief share), or therapy—connection with those who can witness and hold your grief is essential.

The Dual Process Model (Stroebe & Schut)

Healthy grieving involves oscillating between two orientations: "loss-oriented" (facing the grief, crying, missing, processing) and "restoration-oriented" (taking a break from grief, engaging with daily life, adjusting to new circumstances). Moving between both is healthy. Being stuck in only one is a sign that support is needed.

How to Monitor & Support Yourself Through Grief

1. **Grief journaling**– Write to or about what you have lost. Write about your memories, your regrets, your gratitude, your anger. There is no "right" content. The writing itself is processing.
2. **Track the oscillation**– Note when you are in loss-orientation vs. restoration-orientation. Both are needed. If you are stuck in only one for extended periods, seek support.
3. **Create meaningful rituals**– Identify one ritual per month that honors your loss. This provides structure and meaning to an experience that can otherwise feel formless and overwhelming.
4. **Seek grief-specific support**– Many communities have grief support groups that are free and deeply effective. Therapists trained in prolonged grief disorder (CGT) can help if grief remains overwhelming after several months.
5. **Be patient with yourself**– There is no timeline. There is no "over it." There is only "through it"—which is its own non-linear journey. Progress looks like grief becoming more integrated into your story, not absent from it.

A Letter to You

Now that you've heard my story, I want to talk to you.

For this whole book, I've been looking backward and inward—describing what happened to me, what it felt like, how I moved through it. But I didn't write this for me. I already lived it; I don't need a book to remember it. I wrote it for you. So before I close, I want to put the story down and look up, and speak to you directly, whoever you are, wherever you're reading this from.

Because I think I know something about where you might be.

If you picked this book up, there's a chance you're not reading it the way most people read books. There's a chance you're reading it the way I would have—scanning it for proof, looking for someone who has felt what you're feeling, trying to find out if what's happening to you is survivable. Maybe you feel unreal right now. Maybe you feel like you're watching your own life through glass. Maybe you've been checking your own hands, or the shadows of things, or asking yourself over and over if you're okay and never finding an answer that lasts. Maybe you're terrified, in the specific way that's almost impossible to explain to anyone who hasn't felt it, that you are losing your mind.

So let me say the thing I most needed someone to say to me, plainly, before anything else.

You're not losing your mind.

I know you won't fully believe me. I didn't want to believe it either. The disbelief is part of the thing—it argues for its own permanence, it convinces you that you're the exception, that yours is the real one, the different one, the one that doesn't get better. I'm not going to pretend I can talk you out of that in a paragraph. But I can stand here, on the other side of having believed exactly what you believe right now, and tell you that the certainty you feel about losing your mind is a feeling, not a fact. It is the loudest, most convincing feeling I have ever experienced. And it was wrong. It was wrong about me, and I have no reason to think it's telling the truth about you.

Now I want to be honest with you about something else, because you've probably been lied to already, and you deserve better than another comforting lie.

A lot of books like this will promise you that you can go back. That if you do the right things, take the right steps, learn the right tools, you'll return to the person you were before all of this started—that the glass will lift and you'll wake up one morning and it'll be like it never happened.

I'm not going to tell you that, because I don't believe it's true, and I think you can tell when you're being handed a comforting lie.

There is no going back. I'm sorry. I wish there were. I spent a long time waiting to return to a version of myself that I now understand I'm never going to return to. From here, it's only forward. What you're living through is going to become part of you, and it's going to set a new baseline—a new normal that includes what you now know about your own mind, things you can't un-know.

I know how that sounds. When you're in the worst of it,

"you can't go back" sounds like a death sentence. It sounded like one to me. But I've lived in the new baseline long enough now to tell you the part that the death-sentence version leaves out: forward is not worse. It's just different. The new baseline is not the nightmare you're in right now—the nightmare is the transition, not the destination. The new normal, the one you're so afraid of being trapped in, is quieter than where you are tonight. It has bad days, yes. But it also has ordinary days, and it has glimpses, and it has whole hours where you forget to check whether you're real because you're too busy being alive. You are not being sentenced to feel forever the way you feel right now. You're being moved, against your will, to a different place than the one you started in. And that place is more livable than the doorway you're standing in.

So if I can't promise you that you'll go back, what can I actually promise you?

Two things. Only two. But I would stake everything I have on both of them.

The first: you can carry this and still live.

Not "you'll be cured and then live." Carry it and live. At the same time. I know that's not the promise you want—you want it gone, not carried. I wanted that too. But I need you to understand that "carry it and live" is not a consolation prize. It's the actual thing. It's what I do now, most days. I carry the numbness, the detachment, the quiet hum of unreality, and I also go to class, and laugh with my friends, and love the people I love, and play a stupid game with a ball in the last of the daylight and feel completely alive doing it. Both things. The carrying and the living, at the same time. You are capable of that even if you can't picture it right now. Especially if you can't picture it right now—because I couldn't picture it either, and here I am doing it.

And the second promise, the one I'd defend with my life: You are not broken.

You are not broken beyond repair. You are not broken at all, actually—you're overwhelmed, and exhausted, and frightened, and in the middle of something enormous, but none of that is the same as broken. Broken implies something that can't work anymore. You're working. You're reading these words. You're still trying, even now, even like this. That's not what broken looks like. That's what surviving looks like, in the moments before you have the distance to recognize it as surviving.

I don't know you. I'll never know most of the people who read this. But I know one thing about you, right now, with total certainty, and I want to leave you with it.

You are still alive.

You are still alive, because you're reading this, aren't you?

Whatever it took to get to this page—however heavy today was, however unreal it all feels, however sure you are that you won't make it through—you made it to this sentence. You're here. The part of you that's afraid of losing yourself is the same part that's still here reading, still looking for a way through, still fighting even when it feels like giving up. That part of you is not gone. It got buried. There's a difference. And it is still, right now, doing the bravest and most ordinary thing a person can do, which is to keep going for one more page, one more hour, one more day.

You don't have to figure out the rest of your life tonight. You just have to do tonight. And then tomorrow, you do tomorrow.

That's the whole plan. It's the only plan I have, and it's kept me here.

Stay.

That's all I'm asking. Not get better by Friday. Not fix it. Not understand it. Just stay—through this page, through this night, through the part that feels like it can't be survived, which it can, because you're already surviving it.

You're not losing your mind.

You can carry this and live.

You are not broken.

And you are still here.

So am I.

Love,

Cannon

Notes From a Full Mind

- "Struggling did not make me unique. It made me human."

- "Fear can become a place. It can become an environment you live inside."

- "Buried beneath the fear, beneath the panic, beneath the endless questions and sleepless nights, I was still there."

- "I was still there. I just hadn't found my way back to myself yet."

- "The possibility that I wasn't broken beyond repair."

- "Healing is often invisible while it's happening."

- "Just enough hope to keep moving. And sometimes, that is where healing begins."

- "Anxiety is a terrible fortune teller. It speaks with complete confidence and almost no accuracy."

- "The harder I searched for proof that I was okay, the harder it became to feel okay."

- "Every answer created another question, and every question created another opportunity for fear."

- "I missed trusting my own mind."

- "The version of yourself that existed before the struggle begins to feel distant, almost like someone you used to know rather than someone you still are."

- "Still me, even when I didn't feel like it."

- "Sometimes you don't notice you've made progress until you look back months later and realize you're standing somewhere you once thought you'd never reach."

- "The moment you begin asking 'how' instead of 'if,' you've already taken your first step toward the other side."

- "What if I weren't losing my mind?"

- "What if this wasn't the end of my life as I knew it?"

- "Not certainty. Not answers. Not control. Just proof, over and over again, that I was still here."

- "There were cracks forming in the certainty of it."

- “And movement mattered.”

- “The story wasn’t ending. In many ways, it was only beginning.”

- “Hope. Not a loud hope. Not a confident hope. Not the kind that suddenly transforms a person’s life. Just enough hope to keep moving.”

When Your Mind Gets Too Loud

This book talks about internal experiences like anxiety, panic, and feeling disconnected from yourself. If anything in these pages feels familiar to what you are going through, it's important to know you don't have to navigate it alone.

Sometimes mental and emotional experiences can feel overwhelming, especially when they start affecting sleep, daily functioning, or your sense of safety in your own mind. If that is happening, reaching out for support is not an overreaction—it's a healthy step.

Support can look like the following:

- Talking to a trusted adult, friend, or family member
- Reaching out to a school counselor or mental health professional
- Speaking with a doctor or therapist about what you're experiencing
- Letting someone know when things feel like they are getting harder to manage alone

If you are in the United States and ever feel like you are in immediate crisis or unable to stay safe, you can call or text **988** to reach the Suicide & Crisis Lifeline. It is available 24/7 and free.

You don't need to wait until things feel "bad enough" to

deserve help. If it is affecting your life, your thoughts, or your sense of stability, that is enough reason to reach out.

And if you are not in immediate danger but still struggling, support is still valid. You are still allowed to ask for help at any point—not just at the worst point.

I don't know you, but I will tell you that you *can* choose how and what you do with what you have—judgment-free from me! -Cannon

About the Author

Cannon W. Stiffler is an author, student, and world champion cheerleader from Ohio. He is the author of *The Truth*, a book exploring identity, belonging, and the experiences of growing up gay, and *My Mind Struggles*, a deeply personal memoir about anxiety, panic, recovery, and resilience.

Known for his honest and vulnerable writing style, Cannon writes about the experiences many people live through but often struggle to put into words. Through his work, he hopes to create the kind of understanding and connection he once needed himself.

Outside of writing, Cannon has earned a world championship in competitive cheerleading and is passionate about leadership, public service, and helping others. He is an aspiring psychotherapist at New York University, and dedicates his future to serving others through their mental health journey.

Whether writing about identity, mental health, or the challenges of growing up, Cannon's goal remains the same: to remind people that they are not alone.

My Mind Struggles is his second book.

To stay up to date with his journey, visit his official website: www.cannonstiffler.com

www.ingramcontent.com/pod-product-compliance
Lightning Source LLC
LaVergne TN
LVHW040514210926
848480LV00005BA/1455
9798234114181